THE PLAIN

Life on Salisbury Plain from the 1890s to the Present Day

CHRIS CORDEN

HALSGROVE
in association with

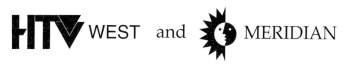

HTV WEST and MERIDIAN

First published in Great Britain by Halsgrove, 1998

Copyright © 1998 Chris Corden

This book is based upon the HTV West and Meridian
television series, *The Plain*, produced by Raw Charm

ISBN 1 87444 898 1

Cataloguing in Publication Data

CIP record for this title is available from the British Library

HALSGROVE
PUBLISHING, MEDIA AND DISTRIBUTION
Halsgrove House
Lower Moor Way
Tiverton
Devon EX16 6SS

Tel: 01884 243242
Fax: 01884 243325
www.halsgrove.com

Printed in Great Britain by Hillman Printers (Frome) Ltd

Contents

For Gill, Tob and Zoë

Foreword

Salisbury Plain, to those who have never been there, is probably the place on the map where Stonehenge is. To others it is mist, mud on the road and the occasional tank. For many in Wiltshire and its surrounding counties, the sound of artillery fire, fast jets and low-flying Hercules are regular reminders of a military presence.

Of course the Plain is all those things, but look around and it becomes much more. On one side you may see a squadron of tanks suddenly cross the skyline like a line of warships making smoke, while on the hill opposite a silhouetted hare pauses, glances at the tanks, dismisses them as no threat, and runs on. The Plain is a magical place, an ancient place, and a place where battles have been fought for thousands of years.

Some readers will recognize names and places from the television series, but *The Plain* is not simply 'the book of the series': it offers an opportunity to look at remarkable old photographs, some of which have never been published before, and amble down a few half-hidden pathways to get a glimpse of the Plain and its people.

For a project that began life as a radio documentary, *The Plain* has taken on a life of its own, largely thanks to Raw Charm, the independent production company who made the television series for HTV and Meridian, and of course the Army, without whose generosity and enthusiasm filming would have been impossible.

This book has involved so many people that individual acknowledgements are impossible. However, special thanks must go to Betty Hooper, the Cole family and the Fuller family, who trusted me with their unique photographs and archives, and Jean Morrison, who sat by her fireside for hours telling me stories of the Plain and its people.

Chris Corden,
Wiltshire, 1998

Stonehenge today

ONE
The 1800s

Salisbury Plain is a place of legend. Merlin is said to have transported the great stones to Stonehenge and there are still those who hear the baying of the 'Wild Hunt' as it rides through the night skies above long-dead villages. The Plain is also a place of warriors. Sometimes man fought man to survive; more often nature was the foe. Since man first walked on the Plain he has farmed and fought. For centuries the world developed slowly. Stonehenge was built, and its purpose was forgotten. Sticks and stones became swords and spears, guns eventually appeared, and killing became more remote.

In 1854 the Light Brigade charged into history against the Russian Artillery at Balaclava and proved, to those willing to listen, that war had changed. Sadly, some in the British Army proved rather deaf. In 1861 a general at the school of musketry told a parade: 'Gentlemen! My unalterable conviction is that the bayonet is the true weapon of the British soldier.'

It is here, in Victorian England, that our tale begins. Prince Albert had just died, the Queen had gone into seclusion, and the British Army was licking its wounds. Training was clearly the answer, but to train a large army required space, which is why large training areas began to be established in various parts of the country. One such area was a sizeable tract of land near Aldershot. It had to be sizeable as in 1871, 32,679 troops used it for a 'large formation exercise'. Those early exercises must have been a logistical nightmare, a nightmare that would have a profound effect on Salisbury Plain, where a similar exercise was held a year later. There were no metalled roads, no running water, no sanitation, no build-

The George, Codford, around 1896. The soldiers in the street had apparently been engaged in exercises on Salisbury Plain.

ings, and everything had to be moved either by hand or 'horsepower'. Added to that, permission was needed from every landowner and farmer whose land was affected. It was a state of affairs that severely hampered military training, and Victorian England was a very militarily active power.

During the 63 years of Queen Victoria's reign there were 36 wars, 18 campaigns, 98 expeditions and 13 operations: a total of 165, which doesn't take into account the numerous rebellions, uprisings, insurrections, and other general disturbances.

It was a level of activity that had already seen the revival of the Volunteer Movement in 1859, with the Reserve Forces Act of 1882 merely confirming the Army's needs, following its defeat in the first Boer War (1880–81).

A general store on Chitterne Road, Codford. Mr Savage, the owner, stands in the doorway. The turnover of such general stores would have benefited from the arrival of the military, though in this shop's case the prosperity was short-lived, as it burnt down in 1902.

Fifteen years later came a Jubilee year for Queen Victoria, and a key year for the Army and many who lived on Salisbury Plain. In 1897 the government signed the Military Manoeuvres Act, described with commendable brevity as 'An Act to simplify military manoeuvres.' It meant the Army could now buy its own land to train on. The shopping spree began on 3 August 1897 with the purchase of Grove Farm in the Parish of West Lavington, on Ball Down. This 364-acre

Durrington, one of the many villages that would eventually feel the effects of the military presence.

The takings of the Dog and Gun on New Road in Netheravon no doubt increased when the Army came to the Plain.

farm cost £3,647 (£10 an acre); no buildings were included in the sale. (In 1998 the land was probably worth between £2,000 and £2,500 an acre, although the original value is said not to have changed much until the Second World War.) The farm is now part of the West Down Artillery ranges.

From this modest beginning the military soon got into its stride, and by the end of 1897 it owned 13,661 acres and had swallowed up a number of large estates. The most important of these was probably Tedworth, not simply because it included Tedworth House; for £95,000 the Army also got 13 farms, 8 farmhouses, 107 cottages, and the Ram Hotel in North Tidworth.

It didn't stop there, of course. Between 3 August 1897 and 31 March 1983 the Army acquired 91,709 acres (37,105 hectares) of land. There were periods when little or no land was bought and others when a great deal was acquired, one increase coinciding with the First World War. Not all the early acquisitions were amicable. Among those to have their land 'compulsorily purchased' were the Ecclesiastical Commissioners, King's College Cambridge, and Winchester College.

Having decided to become major landowners the Army was then faced with the problem of managing it. An early example of military confusion is the tale of Tedworth House. The purchase of the estate was completed on 29 September 1897. Yet at a meeting on 24 May in that same year it had been decided to auction the main house and its contents, 2,200 acres of land, the Ram Inn, and the outlying cottages. However, when the sale was held in July there were no buyers. It was then decided to sell privately, a decision which was revoked in September in favour of finding a tenant.

By January 1898 no tenant had been found, so the Army changed its mind again and decided that, as 'in about twenty years it would be a most valuable property' it would keep it. It was a decision that formed a blueprint for the military's management of its estates in the future, and one that also left it with a lot of cottages.

It was felt that the number and location of the cottages should be recorded, so they were numbered and labelled, not by roads or parishes, but consecutively across the whole of the Plain. The labels, which had a broad arrow with a number underneath, were originally to have been tile labels, until somebody noticed there were between 800 and 900 cottages, whereupon the tiles were replaced by enamelled iron.

Having catalogued and tidied away its human homes, the Army was faced with the problem of another kind of habitat: rabbit warrens. At the end of the last century Salisbury Plain had a huge rabbit population, and rabbit pie was a common supplement to the country diet, both legal and poached. Near The Bustard Inn a 300-acre warren was found surrounded by a wire fence.

To give some idea of the size of the problem, in 1897, 14,000 rabbits were killed on the Tedworth Estate alone. For an army

Historical group members re-enact an 1897 exercise on the Plain.

The church and cottages in Imber around the turn of the century

reliant on horses, rabbit-holes were a serious threat, and the plan was to fill them in by hand. The problem was cost. Someone estimated it would take twenty men a month to fill every hole. Eventually, after six months of inaction, the farm tenants drew the short straw and were told that 'rabbits and their holes' were a farming matter.

Imber

Bought as part of a westward expansion on 27 September 1927, the village of Imber deserves a special place in any 'tale of the Plain'. No living memories remain of late-nineteenth century Imber, where the way of life had remained largely unchanged for centuries. Fortunately, however, there are several written accounts. One is *Salisbury Plain: Its Stones, Cathedral, City, Villages and Folk* by Ella Noyes, illustrated by her sister Dora, and published in 1913. Writing largely of the previous century and earlier, the author opens a window on a vanished world.

With Ella Noyes, the journey to Imber begins at St Joan à Gore Cross. (As she points out, St Joan should actually be St John, as the name records a wayside chapel and the medieval village of Gore.) Gore, or Gare, once stood at what is now the junction of an Army Range Road to Imber and the A361. The current Ordnance Survey map records it as Gore Cross, and just beyond it is the legend 'Robbers' Stone'. This stone commemorates the famous story of Matthew Dean, who was ambushed and robbed as he returned from Devizes market on 21 October 1839. It's a tale that not only reflects the danger travellers faced on the Plain, but the character of those who lived there.

Miss Noyes' account, having passed from many tellers to listeners across the years, is a noble yarn of a single-handed and merciless chase. She writes: 'mile after mile over the open downs where there was no covert or hope of escape, he kept his quarry on the run, this way and that, for three mortal hours, until on Chitterne Down, the hunted man suddenly dropped dead.' Her version leans heavily on the inscription written on the Robbers' Stone. A newspaper court report of the time tells a slightly different, though equally remarkable, story. At the Devizes Sessions, on 31 December 1839:

Richard Harris, George Waters and Thomas Saunders were convicted of a daring robbery upon Matthew Dean, farmer, of Imber, who, on returning from Devizes Fair, 21st October, was attacked by four men near Gore Cross Farm. They pulled him

A general view of Imber from the church

Cottages in Imber that would eventually be owned by the Army

The road towards Warminster in summer

This photograph was almost certainly taken before the First World War, as the windmill on the skyline is said to have collapsed around then. Judging by the washing-lines, it was probably a Monday.

from his horse to the ground; two rifled his pockets, one pressing his nose and mouth to prevent him giving alarm, and the other putting his hand over his eyes. They took from his pocket a pocket book containing £20 notes, and from another pocket one sovereign and a half in gold and £2 in silver. The horse galloped away during the scuffle. Mr Dean on recovering himself followed the men on foot, and within fifty or sixty yards met Mr Morgan of Chitterne, to whom he mentioned the attack.

There then follows an account of Mr Morgan pursuing the robbers on horseback and losing sight of one of them. He kept the other three in view until two labourers joined in and overtook them, but the robbers 'threatened to shoot any man who came near them'. Mr Morgan then thought it was 'prudent to get further assistance, and called on Mr Hooper, who joined the pursuit on horseback.'

As the chase continued across the downs, one of the robbers, a stout man, fell on his back, and the chase continued after the other two. Mr Sainsbury of West Lavington soon joined Messrs Morgan and Hooper in the chase. At last the robbers were cornered and told to surrender. However, as the court report continues:

They were armed with large fold sticks, and threatened Mr Sainsbury if he touched them; upon which Mr Sainsbury, holding up the large end of his hunting whip, said, 'If this is not enough for you, I have a brace of bulldogs [pistols] in my pocket, and if you make the least resistance I will shoot you dead on the spot.' The fellows then surrendered, the pursuit lasted for three hours. The pocket book was found on the down, and the notes safe. On the following morning the fourth man was discovered a corpse on the very spot he was seen to fall.

At the inquest the jury returned a verdict of felo-de-se, which, as Mr Coroner Whitmarsh explained, refers to one who 'deliberately puts an end to his own existence, or commits an unlawful act the consequence of which is his death.' The jury was so pleased with the 'manly conduct of Mr Morgan they entered into a subscription' to buy him a piece of plate.

Waters, Saunders and Harris were found guilty, and Saunders 'was very violent, and swore that if he had a knife he would have "run'd it through Mr Dean".' He calmed down and the three 'acknowledged that, if they were to be hung, they would say they had a fair trial.'

They didn't hang, but were sentenced to fifteen years' transportation and embarked for Hobart on 5 September 1840, arriving on 5 February 1841.

The Robbers' Stone

Highway robbery was an ever-present danger on the lonely roads and tracks across the Plain, and the solitary traveller ventured there at his peril. Happily, there seem to have been no significant robberies after the one on Farmer Dean, probably because banks were set up in the market towns where farmers could deposit their 'market money'.

Farmer Dean was attacked just before he turned his gig off the main road and climbed south-west toward Imber. In 1839 the surface of the main road would have been hard, but the routes to villages were turf tracks. The old rhyme 'Imber on the down, five miles from any town' describes Imber perfectly. Even in Miss Noyes' time the road was a turf track for some of the way. She writes:

The village lies in a deep fold of the Plain, on the track of another little winter stream; on all sides the slopes of the high downs surround it. It is just one straggling street of old cottages and farmsteads, winding along the hollow under the sheltering elms; the narrow stream brims fresh and clear through it in spring, leaving its bed dry, to fill up with coarse grass and weeds in summer. The white-washed cottages, with their leaning timbers and deep thatched roofs, are set down in short rows and groups, the angles and nooks between them filled in with garden plots full of flowers; rose bushes, here and there a lilac, lilies, and tangles of everlasting peas. There is an old timbered house about midway along the street which cannot be younger than the fourteenth century. Such barns too, there are, deep, lofty, capacious, built of grand old timbers, with a thick cape of thatch thrown over the long roof and two pockets in the thatch bulging out over the big double storied doors. The long walls of the orchards and gardens are all the old mud built kind here, rustic and comfortable under their coping of thatch.

Granny Staples' Cottage, 'about midway along the street ... cannot be younger than the fourteenth century.'

'The village lies in a deep fold in the Plain.' Imber, seen from the Heytesbury Road

Barns at Imber: 'deep, lofty, capacious, built of grand old timbers, with a thick cape of thatch'

An Imber cottage, 'rustic and comfortable' under its thatch

Thanks to Jean Morrison from Bratton, a recording exists that also takes us back to the late 1880s. In 1982 Mrs Morrison recorded conversations she had with a Miss Tinnams, who was approaching her hundredth birthday. (It is quite possible that Ella Noyes saw the eight-year-old Alice Tinnams playing while she wandered through Imber in 1890, making notes for her book.) Jean has lived in her cottage in Bratton for the last 40 years, having originally come from the other side of the Plain. She was born in 1912, and has clear memories spanning this century from the First World War to the present day.

Giving an even greater impression of a vanished world than Miss Noyes' account, the tapes reveal Imber to have been an isolated community very much at peace with itself. There were small village shops, a pub, and a blacksmith. On Saturdays the village carrier would go to Warminster, taking any villagers who wanted to go, and a shopping list from others. At the cart's return on Saturday evening a temporary shop would be set up for people to buy what they'd ordered. Then there was the baker in Chitterne who delivered bread and cakes. Chitterne cakes were eaten when the villagers sat down at long trestle tables in the new barns to celebrate Queen Victoria's Diamond Jubilee in 1897.

Alice Tinnams' mother shared a bakehouse with the people next door, and when her father became farm manager up on Southdown she shared one with the carter's wife and the shepherd's wife, taking it in turns to heat the oven. The children would wait around for a 'scalder' to eat and keep watch for the lardy cakes, baked to use up the remaining heat of the oven.

For the young Tinnams, three boys and four girls, school ended at the age of ten, when they started work. Alice remembers playing 'Kissing in the ring' with other village children the day her mother came to take her to her first job.

She earned £4 a year as a maid on a farm in Imber in 1892, and even though her board and lodging was paid for, her mother had to buy her clothes. After a couple of years, and much to her mother's disapproval, she gave in her notice and went to work in Trowbridge. She later moved to London, but returned to Imber during the First World War to look after her mother.

The church at Imber, as painted by Buckley in 1807

The Revd James Hugh Pearson, Vicar of Imber from 1885 to 1889, pictured sitting in his donkey cart with his garden boy beside him and his housekeeper, Mrs Payton, holding the donkey's bridle

Alice Tinnams told Jean Morrison how, up on the Plain, a shepherd used to tell stories from the Bible to men from the village. After a while, they decided to build a chapel. Many, including Alice's father, provided the stone. Alice's recollection is that a wealthy lady from Imber gave them the land to build the chapel, but other records state that it was built, in 1835, at a cost £238.12s.8½d., on the same site as an earlier chapel.

Alice's story of the shepherd is supported by numerous stories about David Saunders, 'The Shepherd of Salisbury Plain'. Among those he is said to have influenced were Reg Hume and Shute Barrington, who were granted a licence for the Baptist Church in 1788. (As a footnote to the story, according to Alice when the benefactress died she was buried under the chapel altar.)

The two churches didn't represent the whole range of worship in the village. Around the turn of the century Mr and Mrs Ware used to bring their horse and wagon to Imber to

Mr and Mrs Davis lived in the cottage with the decorative brickwork

Mr Andrew Davis, Baptist Deacon in 1886, and his wife

Mr and Mrs Ware's meeting-tent, 1909

Missionary meeting

preach the Gospel. They would erect their marquee and stay for about a fortnight. Their visits incensed Mr Watling, the vicar, whose congregation went straight to the meeting-tent on leaving the church.

Another of Alice Tinnams' memories is of two cousins riding on horseback into Imber to say farewell before setting off to fight in the second Boer War (1899–1902). The cousins, one of whom came from Chitterne, the other from Imber, were both Deans, an old Imber family. The Dean family was believed to descend from King John through his mistress, Mollie, whose son became Earl of Gloucester. Only the Imber cousin survived to return from the war.

Frank (Robert Francis) Dean served in the Imperial Yeomanry during the Boer War. Severely wounded in 1900, he was discharged in 1901.

TWO

A New Century Dawns: 1900–1914

Larkhill on 5 December 1914, with the military railway in the background

Amesbury to Larkhill Military Line in 1915. The engine is an 060 Westminster Saddle Tank Engine, no. 1378, made by Peckett & Sons in 1914.

The Military Presence in the Edwardian Era

As Imber saw the dawning of a new century with little sign of change, the Army was learning new skills while fighting against the Boers. War photographers chronicled the conflict so those in Britain could see what was happening.

In 1901 the death of the Queen brought the Victorian era to an end, and the Edwardian era arrived.

In the first week of September 1898, 50,301 troops had exercised on and near Salisbury Plain. In 1904, manoeuvres to practise defending the country against a seaborne force were held in Essex, but in 1907 and 1908 the Plain once again echoed to the sound of military manoeuvres.

These military excursions across the Plain had not gone unnoticed by the railways. Rail travel was well established in the region, having begun when The Great Western Railway built the Westbury to Warminster line in 1851. Other lines and other companies soon followed, but no lines directly connected the growing military centres.

The Great Western wanted to build the Pewsey and Salisbury Light Railway. Their application was refused as, according to the Army, it would 'neutralise, if not entirely destroy the instructional value, in the military sense, of the River Avon,' a decision more than justified when the British Army faced the Boers across the Modder and Tugela Rivers.

Nevertheless, railway lines were built. A branch line from Ludgershall to Tidworth was running by 1901, and the Amesbury and Military Camp Light Railway opened in 1902. Many more were to follow as the military presence, and its need for supplies and construction workers, increased.

Such was the growth in traffic that eventually the income from Tidworth Station exceeded all the other Midland & South Western station receipts put together. Horses were transported by rail, as was a vast amount of coal. Complete Army units travelled by train, three wagonloads of flour arrived every week from Avonmouth, and a meat train came once a fortnight.

The general population also noticed the military presence, though not all took the Army's activities seriously, as the following extract from a pamphlet published in 1907 shows; entitled 'The Military Manoeuvres', it was written in Wiltshire dialect by Edward Slow of Wilton under the pen-name of 'Measter Benjamin Sloper':

Tha plan as vur as I can see is this. Tha Invadin Army (Blue), ten thousand strong, under Zir Ian Hamilton, is zappoused to have landed at Malberer, an is gwain ta march right acroos Zalsbury Plaain ta try an Konker tha Defenden Army (Rid), we about tha seam number a troops under Zir Frederick Stopvird, who is hurrien up from down Bournemouth way to stop tha invaders an drave em back inta tha sae agaen.

Major military events have long been a spectator sport. There are countless accounts of whole populations turning out to watch battles, and many prints show sightseers grouped on hillsides having picnics while battle was joined below. Wiltshire folk had no battles to watch; instead they regularly turned out to watch march pasts and royal reviews.

In 1872, 30,000 troops marched past the saluting dais at Beacon Hill, watched by people who had come from as far away as Salisbury, a 20-mile walk away. In 1898 the salute was taken at Boscombe, where 50,000 troops took part. The parade, which formed up at Porton Down, took two and half hours to pass the saluting base and was described as 'the review of the century'. 'Mrs Brown at the Review' was published afterwards, price one penny:

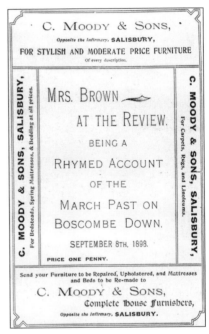

Advertisement for 'Mrs Brown at the Review'

Oh 'Liza, listen unto me,
I be so tired, that I be,
And yet my tongue it won't bide still,
Fyr tell 'ee where I've been I will.
We've been up top o' Boscombe Down
About three mile fra' Amesbury Town,
An there we seed a splendid sight,
A hundred thousan' soldiers quite

A marching by so gallantly:
Sit down and have a cup o'tea
And I will tell you what I've seen
At Boscombe Down where I have been.
Now Farmer Jones he lent his wagon
And two girt horses fur to drag 'en
And give his men a holiday
To have a lark once in a way.
And so my 'usband says to me
He'd take us all this sight to see.
Well, twenty-five of us and more

Left 'ome soon after a' past four
And druv and druv till a'past ten
We never reached that spot till then
For Tom the carter didn't know
Whatever way 'e ought to go,
And when we got there, some did say
We'd come ten mile out o' the way;
But there, it was a lovely ride
Tho' it did shake up my inside.
We found a finger post at last
A'pointin' to the Grand March Past,

And then so many traps in sight
We knew that we was goin' right:
Fur we see'd many a coach an' four
Of Lords and Duchesses I'm sure,
An' two-wheel traps, and covered vans,
And donkey carts, and charaban's,
Carriers, prams, and breaks and pairs,
And parties walkin', and bath chairs,
And some on horses fine did ride,
While bicycles all round we spied.
At last we got up to the place,

An extremely rare photograph of a military review in the late 1800s, thought to be either at Boscombe Down in 1898 or at Beacon Hill in 1872. The very slow shutter speed has blurred the marching troops.

But where to find an empty space
Fur to pull up, we couldn't say,
We seemed in everybody's way.
There was a most tremendous crowd,
All round us, we were not allowed
To bide where first we stopped, they said
We 'ad to draw close up instead
Behind some more concerns where we
Nothing at all of the sight could see.
So then and there we all jumped down:
I nearly tore my black silk gown
By 'itching it up on the shaft,
And lor' how all the people laughed
To see me caught up in the air,
But I were nearly killed, I were,
And that black silk, it is that good
It never tore – you'd think it would.
Well, safely landed on the ground,
Me and my 'usband somehow found
Our was through all the people, right
Up to the rails, and had a sight
Of that magnificent grand review
As if we'd paid a poun' or two
To see them soldiers marching by,
It made me feel inclined to cry.
A 'thinking as they soon may be
All killed in wars defending we –
Why some was only bits o' b'ys,
I'm sure I 'ad to wipe my eyes.
But oh them bands was somethin' fine
A 'playin' all along the line,
And 'Liza dear, it was a treat
To see move their 'ands and feet.
Some was on horseback, some did ride
In carts wi' guns up by their side.
Their clothes was somethin' lovely too
'Twas clear that they was all bran' new.
Fur some wore 'ats o' shinin' gold,
Some banners in their 'ands did 'old,

Some was in red, and some in blue,
And some wore petticoats – 'tis true –
So short they shewed their naked knees,
Quite brazen-faced too, if you please.
But best of all that I did see
Was our own Wiltshire Yeomanry,
All upon hosses dressed so smart,
An' sittin' straight as any dart,
'Twas plain that they was gallant men,
I never seed their like again.
But 'Liza now I'm sure you'll stare
To hear the Queen's own son was there
Among the rest on Boscombe Down
Far from his home in London town.
Well it was nearly a' past two
Before they'd done that great review
And it was gettin' on fur three
When all our merry company
Was up into the cart once more
And startin' home for our own door.
We got back quicker than we go'ed
Because you see we knew the road,
And should a' bin 'ome sooner still,
But comin' down an awful hill,
A girt big hoop come off the wheel,
Lor' how Poll Musselwhite did squeal!
We stopped a 'alf-a-'our quite
Before that they could put it right
And it was gettin' on fur eight
Before we reached our garden gate
But 'Liza dear, 'ow glad I be
To sit and drink this cup o' tea.

The beginning of this century saw the death of Queen Victoria, Edward VII's accession to the throne and the return of the victorious survivors of the second Boer War, who came home as heroes. In Imber there was little change, but the vast construction projects in Tidworth provided work for an army of skilled and unskilled men. While Imber's shepherds drove the Dean's sheep down from high on the Plain to be washed at Bratton, the accommodation at Tidworth improved from tents to barrack blocks.

Eight new blocks were constructed by 1905 and were divided into four Cavalry and four Infantry. The roads in the barrack area were laid out along three roughly parallel lines and named, with military precision, in alphabetical order. Beginning with Aliwal (cavalry), the barrack names commemorated famous battles and sieges in India and Afghanistan. After Aliwal came Assaye (cavalry), Bhurtpore (infantry), Candahar (cavalry), Delhi (infantry), Jellalabad (infantry), Lucknow (infantry) and Mooltan (cavalry).

The Officers' Messes were also completed by 1905, though they lagged slightly behind the barracks, while a Veterinary Hospital was completed by 1904. An interesting omission from the Tidworth plans was a hospital. Although the one established at Bulford in 1905 might have been intended to serve Tidworth, it is tempting to draw the conclusion that horses were valued more highly than men.

The need for a hospital was quickly recognised, however, and in 1907 the Military Hospital Tidworth opened in the former Infantry Barrack Block, Delhi. It was a temporary measure, for as the Matron-in-Chief of Queen Alexandra's Imperial Military Nursing Service reported, following her inspection on 10 May 1908:

No pains have been spared to render the barrack rooms like hospital wards, and to make the patients as comfortable as possible, but it is more than evident that nothing short of a new hospital is required. The number of beds is 120, but these are insufficient for such a large garrison. . . . In the winter it is most difficult to keep the temperature of the wards even as high as 40 degrees Fahrenheit. The ceilings are low and have to be constantly whitewashed as the hanging lamps blacken them.

There was no hot water on the wards and it had to be carried from the kitchen; the Matron-in-Chief was clearly unimpressed. She would have been even less impressed had she know that 23 years later the hospital was still known as Delhi Barracks, Temporary Military Hospital. However, it could be argued that the soldiers had better care than the villagers of Imber. In those days their nearest doctor was in Warminster, as was the chemist, and medical supplies were often vital items on the carter's Saturday shopping list.

As the military population increased, businesses sprang up to serve them, and photographers arrived on the Plain. They did a roaring trade in 'snaps' for soldiers to send back home. Among them were professional photographers like T.L. Fuller. Originally from Tonbridge, Fuller came to take photographs of military and civilian subjects and stayed to establish a unique photographic archive of the Plain. A number of his photographs are reproduced for the first time in this book. Fuller's archive is being continued by his son, who takes many regimental photographs for the Army today.

Fuller's Tonbridge price list

Fuller's cards have now become collectors' items.
Those illustrated here would have been bought by both locals and soldiers.

Top: *Greetings from Salisbury Plain*
Bottom: *George V reviews troops on Salisbury Plain.*

Top: *The village of Ablington*
Bottom: *Netheravon – the clock can still be seen outside the old post office today.*

Top: *A tented camp on Salisbury Plain*
Bottom: *Warminster Camp*

Top: *Early aircraft over Stonehenge*
Bottom: *An event in the grounds of Amesbury Abbey*

Early Developments in Aviation

In the brief Edwardian era strange machines began to appear in the skies above the Plain, including balloons. Observation balloons had been employed during the Boer War, and they were used for some time on the Plain as artillery targets. However, their potential career in the British Army ended almost before it had begun. By 1905, Lieutenant J.W. Dunne of the Wiltshire Regiment had produced a number of gliders, and by 1908 S.F. Cody had flown a powered aircraft at Farnborough.

Despite these breakthroughs, balloon development continued and in May 1909 the Army held trials of its new dirigible at Farnborough. Not a spherical structure, the dirigible now had the cigar shape of the German *Graf Zeppelin*, and the ill-fated British *R101*.

Then, in June 1909, Horatio Barber, a flying enthusiast, rented a small plot of land at Larkhill, not far from the Tombs Road junction with the Packway. There he built a shed for his aircraft, thus starting a chain of events that would lead to the formation of the Royal Flying Corps, and eventually the Royal Air Force.

By the end of 1909 H.C. Barber had been joined by two other flyers, G.B. Cockburn and Captain J.D.B. Fulton, RFA. Captain Fulton, one of the leading pilots of his time, would join the Air Battalion in 1913 and become an instructor at the Central Flying School, Upavon, in 1913. An equally distin-guished future lay ahead for Cockburn, who was described as a 'philanthropic private aviator'; he taught the first four Naval pilots to fly at his own expense.

At roughly the same time that Captain Fulton began parking his Bleriot Monoplane alongside Horatio Barber's new machine, the War Office erected two buildings a short distance south of Larkhill. Development continued in June 1910, when the British & Colonial Aircraft Company built a large hangar to house aircraft from the flying school it had formed. This company later became the Bristol Aeroplane Company, which evolved into the British Aircraft Corpora-tion, today's British Aerospace.

Observation balloon directing the advance on Potgieter's Drift on 16 January 1900, during the Boer War. This illustration, said to be based on a sketch made at the time, comes from With the Flag to Pretoria, *published in 1900 by Harmsworth Brothers.*

Army balloon being inflated at the Bristol Flying School, a base for early aviation on the Plain

Thus airfields joined the barrack blocks, burial mounds and ancient stones of Salisbury Plain, while aircraft joined the buzzards in the skies above. The old stones may have been fortunate to survive the arrival of the airfields; one military flying enthusiast is said to have proposed moving Stonehenge, because it was in line with the end of a take-off runway and 'in the way'. The story may be apocryphal, but the development of flight was viewed with such pride in the district that some would probably have taken the suggestion seriously.

As the *Salisbury and Winchester Journal* reported at the time: 'Salisbury Plain as an aviation centre is increasing in renown and the next few years may see great developments in the art in this district.' This did in fact happen; on 13 May 1912 the Royal Flying Corps was formed. For once logical military thinking failed and No. 3 Squadron (not No. 1 or 2), became the first operational squadron of the RFC. It is now the oldest squadron in the RAF and bears the proud motto 'The third shall be first.'

A month after the RFC was formed, the Central Flying School opened at Upavon, and Wiltshire's place in the history of flight was assured, but it was not to be without casualties.

Card published by T.L. Fuller to commemorate Major Hewetson

On 5 July 1912 Captain E.B. Lorraine, RE, and Staff Sergeant R.H.V. Wilson were killed when their Nieuport Monoplane crashed near the crossroads on the A344 a mile and a half west of Stonehenge. This, the first fatal flying accident on Salisbury Plain, is commemorated by the stone cross which stands at 'Airman's Corner'.

A little over a year later, on 17 July 1913, Major A.W. Hewetson was killed in his Bristol Coanda monoplane at Larkhill as he took the test for his aviator's certificate. More deaths followed, but the future of military flying was secure, both for reconnaissance and directing artillery fire, as the *Salisbury Journal* reported in 1913 when it covered the summer exercises of 1913:

There was a great deal of public interest in flying, though some airshows had tragic consequences. On Sunday, 19 May 1912, sixteen-year-old Leonard Williams of Amesbury was killed when this aircraft ran into the crowd. The pilot, Lieutenant Ashton of the Fourth Dragoon Guards, was unhurt.

Yatesbury, 15 February 1918. Flying remained unpredictable and some landings were better than others.

A very interesting feature was the use of aeroplanes to direct the fire of artillery against a concealed battery.... There were three or four aeroplanes belonging to the military wing of the Royal Flying Corps at the exercise and though there was a fresh wind, they were almost continually at work and sent down constant good reports of the position of the dummies. These reports were thrown down in little bags with streamers attached and orders were sent up to the flying men by cypher in the form of block letters of white canvas, pegged out or laid flat on the ground.

The *Journal* concluded:

As a result there were a few hits on the target and the modest success was striking enough to make it clear that nothing should be spared to continue these experiments and to fit out each brigade of artillery with a supply of planes and fliers.

However, as history relates, it didn't take long for the aeroplane to move from a passive, supporting role to an active, aggressive one.

While the aeroplane took wing across the Plain, another era ended. Edward VII died in 1910, to be succeeded as King of Great Britain and Northern Ireland and Emperor of India by George V.

The king had a naval background, having joined the Royal Navy in 1877, ending an active career in 1903 with the rank of Vice-Admiral. He began his reign using the suffix 'of the house of Saxe-Coburg-Gotha', reflecting the Royal Family's German origins. However, following England's declaration of War against Germany in 1914, the king renounced all the German titles belonging to him and his family and changed the suffix to 'the Royal House of Windsor'.

During the last years of peace, life on the Plain followed the age-old pattern set by the seasons. The villagers of Imber still reached their homes along grassy tracks, drew their water from wells or from the streams, and coped with the occasional winter floods.

Village life remained both self-sufficient and dependent. The community catered for its own needs, but the villagers relied upon each other. The village midwife saw the new villagers into the world, and most probably 'laid out' those leaving it. The blacksmith wrought his craft, teachers taught, vicars preached, and the weather was never quite right for farmers.

It was a village untroubled by world events, an 'upstairs, downstairs' world where people were largely at peace with their lot in life. Alice Tinnams tells of how, when the family killed their pig, the 'gentleman farmer always wanted some'. This is said not to make a point, nor with any outrage, but simply because that's how it was, just as it was natural for her to go into service at the age of ten for £4 a year.

It was also a village that shared. One of Alice's fondest memories was the rook shoot. Every year, farmers from all around the area would come to shoot the rooks, and they would give everyone in the village two or three. As Alice remembered, 'You had to skin 'em and they'd be lovely in a pie.'

Christmas customs

In the first years of the twentieth century, some of the larger farms probably still burned the Christmas Faggot. Our images of traditional country Christmases today are of Christmas trees, Yule logs, carols, and snow. Yet these are Victorian inventions, imported by a German Royal Family used to their own traditions. Trees are scarce on the Plain and certainly not to be wasted by being burnt. Instead, twigs and underbrush were gathered, bound at regular intervals into a faggot, and lit. As the faggot burned, the bindings broke and there was 'a drink and song with every thong'. When the Temperance Movement took hold, the part of alcohol in the ritual would gradually have been dropped.

The Christmas celebrations were not just for the farmer's family; all his workers and their families would be invited. A long table would be set down one side of the kitchen, with a space left for people to dance and watch the faggot burn. If there were a lot of children, a smaller faggot was often burned for them in the afternoon.

Celebrating the coronation of George V at the King's Arms Inn, Amesbury, in 1910

There would be more than enough to eat. The farmers' stock was reduced for the winter and, with no way of storing food for long periods, what wasn't eaten would go bad. As a matter of pride, farmers tried to have beef on the menu to show they were doing well enough to spare a beast for the celebrations.

Traditionally, 'Old Boxing Day' was the day on which the horses were bled, just as today we give blood transfusions to aid recovery.

However, Jean Morrison's theory is that the bleeding was an echo of the sacrifice of the white horse to the moon goddess, an ancient ritual act commemorated in Wiltshire by the white horses scratched out of the chalk hills, some of which date back over 3,000 years.

Imber occasionally had to cope with winter floods, like this one in 1911.

The Dean family at Seagram's Farm, Imber, in 1912

Mills and dew-ponds

Another memory of Alice Tinnams' is Imber's windmill, perched high on Chapel Down behind Tinker's Farm. She remembers the family taking their gleanings to be milled there, the barley being given to their pig and the wheat used to make bread. Thomas Goddard was miller from about 1898 until the mill closed down some time between 1903 and 1910. It continued to be a village landmark until the beginning of the First World War.

The miller before Thomas Goddard was E.H. Dean, while earlier in the century the Cruse family, who moved into the village in 1785, ran the mill. In 1848 James Cruse was both carrier and miller, and Alfred Cruse succeeded him in 1855. But, more importantly, the Cruse family were dew-pond makers.

Among the other dew-pond making families in Imber were the Whites and the Daniels. Charles White, born in 1840, was chief dew-pond maker to the Ecclesiastical Commissioners. His job took him as far as Dover and he built the last dew-pond in Winchester. Closer to home, there were Chettles Pond and Shores Pond, between Imber and Lavington. For some reason both these ponds were named after men who drowned in them.

While one pond was being dug near the windmill above Imber a mass grave was unearthed. It was quickly filled in and another site chosen. It is not known whether the grave's occupants were the victims of battle or plague.

Members of the Cruse family in front of the Imber windmill

The following account of dew-pond making comes from an interview with Charles White and Joel Cruse made shortly before Joel's death in 1923:

Charles White (left) and Joel Cruse, dew-pond makers

When a landowner or a farmer wished to have a supply of water ready to hand, for the purpose of watering his sheep on the downs, he would call to his aid a man who understood the method of making a small reservoir, or dew-pond. A dew-pond is so called because of its dependence upon the natural fall of rain or dew. Dew-ponds are usually made upon the highlands remote from wells or water courses; indeed they would not be wanted in places or situations where there was in the summertime a running stream. For examples of sites, at Sutton Veny, the site of one, when constructed was found to be on a level with the summit of the church spire, and others on the hills surrounding Imber are at 600 feet above sea-level.

The man consulted would be shown the desired situation, and he would be told how many head of sheep were kept, and the sort of size of pond required. A sheep ... [may] drink two gallons of water at one time. Although this man might be unable to proceed to the eleven times table in arithmetic, he could calculate with accuracy, after quiet thought and measurement, the cost of the undertaking and an estimate would be forthcoming.

The farmer or the agent for the property would usually accept these calculations (after he himself had verified them) of a man who had received no more education after he was seven or eight years of age, except for night school. Into his reckoning would come the hire of three assistant men who would be paid at the rate of 18 shillings per week, as a regular wage, upon a given piece of work. Some four weeks would be required for the making of a pond 22 yards or 1 chain square. He would have to provide the necessary tools, such as wheelbarrows, water pots, pickaxes, spades, rakes, prongs, beaters, sieves and a spirit-level (the latter a foot in length, and which for use was tied to a piece of wood 6 feet long, with pegs attached). A beater is especially made with wooden handle and butt, with an iron base. It weighs about 7 lbs. It must be skilfully handled by experienced men. A careless stroke would destroy the surface and render reconstruction necessary.

He would have to reckon it would cost in wages sixpence per yard, for four men together, to remove the earth from the site of a pond of such a size; and another sixpence per yard to fill in the materials for the construction of the floor of the bed. Whatever method he adopted in his own mind he might tender an estimate for £40 and this sum would cover his own profit, the wages of his assistants and wear and tear upon his own tools. In general practice a farmer undertook the removal of the excavated soil, the cartage and the provision of materials.

The work is now commenced by the removal of the soil to a depth of 8 feet. The laying of the floor is then proceeded with from the centre, called the crown, four or five yards in circumference, and to this, each day, a width of about two yards is added, and continued, course by course, until the side of the basin attain to the normal level of the site. Only so much work, with the layers of materials set in order, is undertaken in one day as can be finished by nightfall, and this must be covered over with straw and steaned

Making a dew-pond: Charles White (right), Jim Earley (second left), William Carter and, it is thought, Charles White's brother Robert (left).

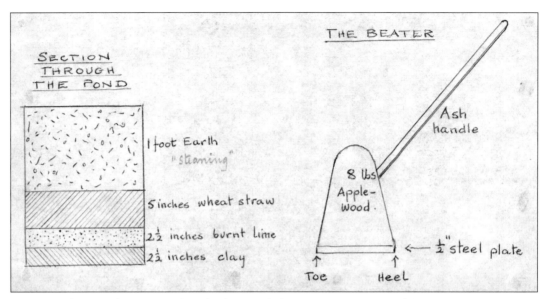

Drawing showing the construction of a dew-pond, from Betty Hooper's archives

(covered with soil). No layering may be done in frosty or inclement weather.

This is the method of construction: 70 cartloads of clay are scattered over the area suggested above. The clay is thoroughly puddled, trodden, and beaten in flat with beaters, a coat of lime spread, slaked, and lightly beaten until the surface is as smooth as a table, and it shines like glass. After it has been hammered in twice, a second coat of lime is applied to the thickness of half an inch, which is wetted and faced to save the under face. A wagonload of straw is arranged, and the final surface is covered with rough earth to the thickness of about nine inches. The pond, when finished, affords a depth of water of seven feet.

The best and hardest sort of lime is the blue stone, and this was used for the Winchester ponds, as it is obtainable there. It was looked upon as being dangerous to the eyes of the workers. In this county the Warminster, or white lime, such as is used in whitewash, is used. Other than the application of a thicker coating with the latter there is little to choose between the two limes.

The pond is then encircled or surrounded by a fence of wood or of iron bolted together. The object of this is to keep away horses or cattle, whose hoofs would break through the bed, and to admit sheep, for the watering of which dew-ponds are made. The pond makers prefer to construct round ponds because less earth has to be removed than is the case with a square, and the soil does not shift too uncertainly. The durability of the dew-ponds, when properly constructed and used, extends to about 20 years. There are ponds in good condition now which were made 36 years ago and have never been known to fail to yield an adequate supply of water, even in the year of the drought, 1921.

Up to ten years ago the dew-pond makers started upon their work about the twelfth of September, touring the country for a period of about six or seven months, making in sequence from six to fifteen according to the size and convenience, in a season of winter and spring; such labour is too exacting in the warmer weather. They travelled throughout Wiltshire and Hampshire, and occasionally they carried their operations into Somersetshire and

Berkshire and even into Kent. Much work was done on behalf of the Ecclesiastical Commissioners. Harvesting claimed their presence in the summer and autumn.

The account continues with a couple of personal observations from the author:

They would be recommended to lodgings and return to them year by year, for in those days the men of Imber were clearly, in person and character, upright, trusty and trustful, and they paid ready money for their simple needs. Henry Wadsworth Longfellow in 'The Village Blacksmith' typifies the personality of our men. For their lodgings they paid 2/6 weekly for five nights, for sleeping accommodation and their cooking, returning home for Saturday and Sunday. They provided their own food.

The reason for the decay of the industry is said to be the advent of the water pump, which is driven by the wind, and pumps from wells; and to a certain extent it is due also to the unwillingness of men to engage in work of so laborious a nature, for less than a higher rate of payment which cannot be met by landowners or farmers.

Joel Cruse was the youngest of seven children. Some of the boys left school at the age of seven and all were helping in the family business by the time they were ten. Eventually two left the land to join the police force, one joining the Somerset Constabulary, the other the Wiltshire.

Henry Cruse joined the Wiltshire Police in 1840, when he was 26, and served for 30 years. At the time of his death in 1935 he was described as 'the oldest police pensioner in Great Britain' and the last survivor of the 'peelers' – the constabulary formed by Sir Robert Peel. Henry Cruse may have left school early, but he reached the rank of Inspector.

Like many a Plainsman before him, he had a large family. At the time of his death, two weeks before his ninety-fifth birthday, he had 60 descendants. These included six children, 22 grandchildren, 27 great-grandchildren and a great-great-grandchild.

Joel Cruse and his wife Elizabeth. Joel was born on 13 December 1842 and Elizabeth on 15 February 1845. They died within nine days of each other, Joel on 19 February 1923 and Elizabeth on 28 February.

Henry Cruse, 'last of the peelers'

THREE

The First World War: 1914–18

Codford

South across the Plain from Imber is the much less isolated village of Codford, which is actually two villages, Codford St Mary and Codford St Peter. They lie in a line on the north side of the Salisbury Road in the Wylye Valley.

The experiences of this community during the two world wars, reflected in many other places around the Plain, are preserved in a remarkable first-hand account by Harry Cole; never published, it is called 'The Village: 1914–64'. The Cole family moved from South London to Wiltshire in 1914. Harry was a water engineer with Babcox and Wilcox and was sent to erect pumping stations for military camps. The photograph on the following page shows the Codford pumping station being built in 1914/15. It was opposite the railway station and Wessex Water confirm that the borehole is still in use today.

The family first settled in Stapleford, moving to Codford in 1919. In Codford, Harry began to breed Wessex Saddleback pigs. Three years later Codford Mayflower, a gilt, won the Royal Bath and West Show at Romsey. He sold her for 365 guineas, a record price for a gilt that stood until 1952. Harry used the money to buy the land he had been renting and he renamed it Mayflower Farm.

In 1924 he began writing Salisbury Market reports for the Ministry of Agriculture and Fisheries. These were published in local newspapers and were soon joined by district news reports in the *Warminster Journal, Wiltshire Times*, and *Western Gazette*. He retired from farming in 1970, and in 1974 was awarded the British Empire Medal for the 50 years he had spent writing market reports. He died 1981 at the age of 93, having contributed to local newspapers as an area correspondent until he was 90.

The following is a description Codford around the time of the First World War, as seen through the eyes of Harry Cole:

Among the twenty or so villages which lay in this lovely valley of the River Wylye from Wilton to Warminster, Codford would not perhaps be counted among the most beautiful. It has none of the old-world charm of neighbouring Stockton, or the unspoiled rural setting of Sherrington which make them so much more attractive and desirable to people seeking rural retreats. Parts of it may lay claim to beauty, especially round the fine stone bridge over the river just inside the park, and the area around the nearby ford from which the place probably takes its name – *Co-ed-ford*, the wooded ford – where there are some fine trees, as indeed there are in other parts of the village although in 1914 there were many more. In Doomsday Book the name is written 'Coteford'.

Codford has no fine old manor house, such as Stockton House or Boyton. In fact the Lords of the Manor of Codford were the Yeatman Biggs family of Stockton, nor has it any predominating residence new or old to give it distinction. Even the new housing areas developed since the last war cannot be said to have

Codford pumping station under construction in 1914 or 1915

contributed anything of aesthetic value to the place. There are some nice Georgian and early Victorian houses, mostly hidden from view by walls and hedges, and the smaller houses, chiefly in the main street are with few exceptions, built right up to the road frontage. A pair of old cottages opposite St Peter's Church, so built, are not without interest. On the wall facing the road is the date 1722 and the letters I.C. The story goes that Isaac Crouch, who owned the property and lived in the adjoining house, had two daughters, who quarrelled continually about a lover. Unable to stand the repeated bickering over the swain, who did not settle the matter by marrying one of them, he had the two cottages built and put one daughter in each.

The village would appear to have grown haphazardly (having two parishes might have had something to do with this), and straggles alongside the main road, which narrows badly at the lower end, where the Chitterne brook runs under the road to join the Wylye. St Peter's Church in a fine position at the top of the hill is situated quite close to the highway whilst St Mary's Church is tucked away at the lower end of the village under the curve of the Downs and adjoins East Farm House. This house is on the site of an ancient hermitage, and the stone fireplace from it now forms the porch of Mr Frank Sykes's house at Stockton. To the end of 1914 it was just a typical Wiltshire village with two parishes, two churches and a chapel, with at that time considerable congregations attending them all. A school in each parish where the children went until they were old enough to leave. There was only one public house, the George Inn, now called an Hotel. At one time the Brewery was behind the Inn, and stood on the ground which has become the garden. The water was drawn from a well now behind a pair of cottages. There is also an off-licence which sold beer only for six days of the week.

The carrier's van went once weekly to Salisbury, and twice to Warminster. In 1914, a carrier started a Motor Carrier Van service from Chitterne to Salisbury which picked up at Codford. The van

Codford camps under construction

Codford's No. 5 Camp under canvas was built very close someone's croquet lawn.

The railway ran into No. 6 Camp.

had solid tyres, and transported live and dead stock as well as passengers. There were at that time only two cars in the village. The Doctor drove on his rounds in a pony and trap. There were bicycles of course, and the railway with the station over a mile from the village. The post went to the station on a hand cart late in the evening, pulled and pushed by two men, or three if the post was heavy. The shops consisted of two grocers, a draper, butcher's, saddler, cycle shop and blacksmith. No telephone or electric light – coal was 24s. per ton, rent and rates were low. Income Tax if you paid any was 1s.2d. in the pound, and food was cheap. Housewives for the most part were careful, thrifty and hardworking – they had no modern amenities such as piped water or washing machines. They did have a store of practical knowledge and made the little money they had to go round, by a host of well-proved methods of making ends meet, e.g. a pig in a sty, jam making, home remedies in cases of illness, wine making (lovely stuff some of it) and mead, potent and palatable. Cider was made locally, although rather rough.

Much of the children's clothes were made at home, and new clothes were mostly made to last. Skirts were long, and the rest of the ladies' garments were substantial and voluminous. The young girls made the best of themselves, but cosmetics and make-up were not used. For a girl to use lipstick or nail-varnish would have branded her as someone better not to know. Girls up to fourteen or fifteen wore their hair long and their greatest pride were long curls done up each night in curling papers.

Men were for the most part soberly and solidly clad. Moustaches, and whiskers of all shapes, colours and sizes were worn by older men, but they were on the way out. This solid and staid habit of dress was reflected in their deportment. People of forty or so were elderly, and at sixty seemed quite old. Perhaps it was the life of manual work that began earlier which aged people quickly. On the whole life proceeded at a leisurely pace; they fed the chickens, milked the cows, ploughed the fields and scattered, then they had a pint or two at 'The George' on Saturday (2d. a pint) and went home to bed. On Sundays, they went to church or chapel,

Codford's hospital camp, where many overseas troops died without ever hearing 'the monstrous anger of the guns'.

paid proper respect to Squire and Parson, looked the whole world in the face, and owed not any man.

The abnormal rainfall of late 1914 and early 1915 had caused considerable flooding in the village and the area from the Park Lodge to the west of Chitterne Road was under water. The ford had disappeared and the footbridge was impassable. The land round the station, into which from late 1914 large numbers of men and vast quantities of materials for camps were poured, was churned by horses, carts and traction engines into a quagmire which had to be seen to be believed. The flooding which had occurred over the whole area of Salisbury Plain had brought about a condition on the roads with which the local authority had neither the equipment or resources to cope, and the place quickly earned unenviable notoriety as 'Codford-on-the-Mud'.

It was to Codford that the First World War brought all the traffic of a military camp, and the main road that at that time was totally unsuited for any heavy volume of traffic rapidly became a sea of mud. Over the plain, the consequences of the flooding were much more serious. Large numbers of troops from overseas (mostly Canadians) trained under appalling conditions, and many died

from Cerebro-spinal Meningitis, brought on, it was said, by the wet and cold. Whatever the cause, many who left their homes in distant parts of the Empire to fight for the Motherland left their bodies in her care in England without having seen the battlefields of Flanders, or heard, to quote Wilfred Owen, 'what passing bell for those who die as cattle, only the monstrous anger of the guns'.

Billets on the Plain

The north and west of the Plain also took its toll on the troops, for although the weather had been warm and dry during September 1914, the arrival of the first Canadian and Newfoundland troops heralded a dramatic change. One contingent of divisional troops arrived at Patney Station, roughly half-way between Westbury and Hungerford, shortly after midnight on 21 October. They were bound for the camp at Pond Farm and must have thought it an apt name, for their three-hour night march to the camp marked the break in the weather. Between their arrival in 1914 and the middle of February the following year, some 24 inches

Soldiers and supply wagons negotiating difficult conditions at Larkhill

of rain fell, an average of about an inch every five days.

The troops were under canvas, there was nowhere to dry their kit, and it rapidly became clear that huts were needed. Huts take time to build, and by Christmas 1914 there were still 11,000 Canadians living under canvas. Therefore, in January 1915 the mounted troops and artillery were moved into billets in places like Bratton, Erlestoke and Market Lavington. This left only the First Canadian Infantry Brigade under canvas.

It may be this exercise Gladys Sutton (née Dean) describes in her reminiscences about soldiers being billeted in Imber Court: 'There were 40 soldiers in the attic, six batmen the other end, a Major and five officers.' Gladys and one of the maids used to give them tea at 6 a.m. before they went out.

On 4 February 1915 the troops were reviewed by George V, accompanied by Lord Kitchener. Three days later, they began to leave for Avonmouth and passage to France. There were delays and the crossing was rough but, as one report said, 'There was little complaining, for present inconveniences were offset by the general feeling of relief at leaving the misery of Salisbury Plain.'

The situation at Larkill seems to have been little better. On 3 September 1916, W.J. Sinney almost certainly echoed many a commonwealth soldier's feelings when he wrote:

It has been raining like fun here and things about Lark Hill are pretty sloppy. It's a rotten place when it rains and a jolly sight worse if it keeps fine for any length of time. The dust is that fine that it will get in anywhere; do what you will, you can't get away from it.

Floods on Countess Road, Amesbury, January 1915

Troops arriving at a rail-head on Salisbury Plain

George V and Lord Kitchener review Candadian troops shortly to depart for France, 4 February 1915.

It wasn't just the commonwealth military who took a dim view of conditions on the Plain, even if they were in hutted camps. Men of the 2/5th Battalion of the Gloucestershire Regiment have left us a vivid glimpse of life in 1916:

On the night of February 19th, the Battalion reached Tidworth and marched to its headquarters at Parkhouse Camp. First impressions of life on the Plain were not very encouraging: the weather was bitterly cold; there were no palliasses [straw mattresses]; there were no fires and no light as the electricity failed on the night of the Battalion's arrival. The men were put into huts, given rations and three blankets apiece and left to get what sleep they could on bare bed-boards.

There followed three months of route marches, field-days, exercises, rifle practice and trench digging until, on 5 May, the men of the Battalion were inspected by the king:

We marched off at 9 a.m. It was close and muggy, but rain during the previous night had laid the dust. As the inspection had been well organized, it was not so long drawn out as most operations of a similar nature. It was a most impressive sight. Twenty thousand men, hundreds of horses and wagons all moving together in an endless line, under the command of a single man – all very fine, fixed bayonets, drawn swords and bands playing. One does not wish to be a pessimist, but I couldn't help wondering how many would come back alive from France.

On 24 May 1916 they boarded the train at Tidworth Station to travel to Southampton, before embarking for France:

The Battalion had arrived on the Plain under the worst possible conditions, but despite the discomforts and the tedium of training, Parkhouse Camp had quickly become its home, and though doubtless no one was sorry for a change of venue, yet when the day of departure arrived, there was a feeling of reluctance to leave the Plain and the memories it held in its undulating folds.

The Plain was to see many such arrivals, followed by many such departures. Whole families of men would leave, indeed whole villages of fighting men would leave to join their county's regiment and head for France.

'It was a most impressive sight. Twenty thousand men, hundreds of horses and wagons all moving together in an endless line under the command of a single man.'

Lord Kitchener (right) on one of his regular visits to the Plain

Some soldiers would take with them a memory of Stonehenge on a midsummer's dawn.

Soldiers resting near what is now the busy A303, bearing off to the left, and the A344 to Devizes

Top-secret research

An agricultural engineering business had thrived in Bratton through most of the nineteenth century. In the forefront of the technology of the time, it exhibited in Paris and Brussels, and at such events as the Great Exhibition of 1851. Among the firm's products were transportable water tanks, used to take water out to livestock on places like Salisbury Plain. At the beginning of the war, the government asked them to try out a new weapon, a large metal vehicle on tracks.

It was a top-secret project, but Bratton was a small village, and a huge vehicle clanking along the narrow lanes could hardly be missed; a cover story was needed. The answer was simple: they let it be known that it was an experimental water tank for taking water on to the Plain, which is how the tank got its name.

The Impact of 'The Great War'

Harry Cole's account is a poignant record of the effects of the military occupation and the First World War on small communities such as Codford on Salisbury Plain:

'Special trains brought workmen out each day from Salisbury to work on the camps.'

Recuperating soldiers outside one of the hospital buildings at Codford

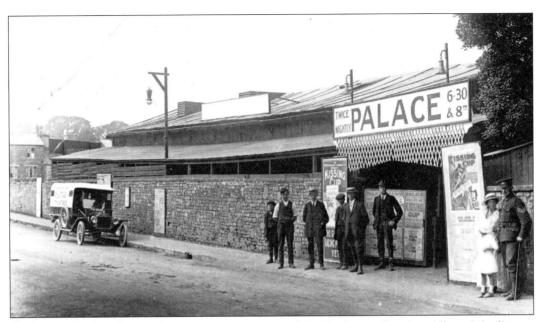

The Albany Picture Palace, Codford, in 1915. The Model-T Ford van advertises Albany Ward's Military Theatre and Albany Ward himself stands in the doorway wearing a straw hat and knee-breeches.

Mud was everywhere. Newly enlisted men were under canvas here and there in the area, and the need for better quarters than tented camps was vital and urgent. Water supplies were negligible and contaminated by flood water. The contractors had recruited hundreds of men from all parts of the country to help in the building of proper accommodation. Special trains brought workmen out each day from Salisbury to work on the camps, and all sorts of temporary huts and buildings were being erected anywhere and everywhere to provide for the invading army of soldiers and civilians. It seemed like chaos, and it was – fifteen camps to be built as well as a hospital and its accompanying buildings. R.E, A.S.C. and the necessary services such as stabling, water supply, electricity, drainage, etc., all had to be erected and installed without any of the present-day equipment for trenching and building. It was done by hand, pick and shovel, and muscle power. A branch railway line was run from the siding at the station to near East Farm and northwards. Horses, carts and steam waggons did the hauling, ropes and tackle did the lifting, and some shape of things to come emerged. The village was submerged in the feverish activity of preparation for waging war on a scale hitherto unknown. Gunfire surrounded it, indeed was in it.

In the main street every vacant plot including front gardens, where there were any, sprouted temporary shops, cafés, barbers, tobacconists, photographers, grocers, butchers, boot and shoe shops, chemists, and tailors. The Wool Stores, a legacy to the village of an industry long transferred to Yorkshire, became a cinema, complete with orchestra pit. The reading room where chess was once regularly played became a café. At the rear of St Mary's Church a huge Army Institute was put up, and various religious organisations all had provision for the spiritual welfare and social needs of the men who were there, and still coming. In fact,

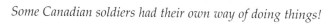
Some Canadian soldiers had their own way of doing things!

English riders taking a more sedate approach to the ford, Codford.

Winter in Codford in the First World War

Codford had all the accessories and equipment of a fair-sized town, and that is what it was, with inhabitants of every type.

The first occupants were English troops newly enlisted, full of enthusiasm and patriotic fervour, men from all walks of life – with but one object: to get to France as quickly as possible. As more of the camps became available, men from overseas began to fill them. They came from distant parts of the Empire: Australians, great big men, rough and ready; undisciplined by our standards but great fighters and eager to be in the war. They had little respect for law and order, and they left the 'George' a shambles after one hectic evening, but as fighters (and the First World War was a fighting man's war) they were superb. Of a similar type, but quieter in manner and tidier in appearance, more amenable to discipline, were the New Zealanders. They were fine men too, tall, but lighter in build than the Australians. A few South Africans were also stationed here.

These were the inhabitants of the camps from 1915 to the end of the war. Their number at its peak was ten to eleven thousand but decreased as time went by.

In the middle of this frenzied activity and conglomeration of people was the village. Who lived in it you did not know – what they did or where they worked was also unknown – that it had any life of its own nobody could say; its entity disappeared. Certainly some farming was going on, but in a limited way by few older men. Many of the younger men had gone away, so farming activity was curtailed. In addition, all the best horses and large quantities of hay and corn had been requisitioned for the use of army transport. Never had the village seen such mule teams as came to Codford, some of them 16 to 17 strong. Dairying was restricted to a few small cow-keepers.

Looking back on the military occupation, one now realizes that a fundamental change was taking place, not only in Codford but in the country as a whole. It was as if a shutter had been pulled down on the old order, to be raised five years later on a new. Whether a better one was a question to which no answer was possible, but changes were going on. Although the upheaval in the pattern of daily life was accepted, including the disappearance of Sunday as a day of rest, the seed of a new set of values had been sown.

FOUR
Peace Once More: 1918–39

At the end of the First World War, Codford had materially changed. There were new buildings, new businesses, new people even, and there were the military graveyards. All over Wiltshire the observant traveller will come across neat ranks of white graves. Each of the stones, simply inscribed with name, date and regiment, has its own story, and each group is a piece of history. Some men died from wounds received overseas or during training; a large number died in the great influenza epidemic after the war.

Twenty-seven men of Imber had gone to fight in the Great War; three were killed and another three were wounded. All are commemorated on a memorial erected near the blacksmith's shop. But there were crops to sow and animals to

The War Memorial at Imber, commemorating the men of the village who fought in the Great War. Those killed were: E. Marsh (France), A. Norris (Gallipoli) and H.H. Kitley (France). Those who served were: A. Bundy, L. Carter, N.D. Carter, W. Carter (wounded), W.I. Carter, P.A. Daniels, H. Daniels, L.L. Daniels, F.J. Daniels, H.W. Daniels, E.H. Daniels, T.L. Daniells, H.T. Dean, H. Goddard, W.W. Grey, A.J. Grey, R.A. Kitley (wounded), R.W. Meaden, W.A. Pearce (wounded), J.V. Potter, H. Potter, F. Palmer, R. Tinnams, L.P. Tinnams and W. White.

The military cemetery at Durrington

feed; the seasons didn't stop just because there'd been a war. Farming would resume until another war disturbed the open downs, burrowing rabbits and grazing sheep.

A Shepherd's Life

Sheep were the main source of manure on many farms, before it began to arrive in sacks from chemical companies, which made the shepherd one of the most important men on the farm. At Imber the four-field system was used to rotate the crops, with grain crops being grown in only two years out of the four. The other two years the land produced a mixture of swedes, kale, rape and turnips, or was left to grass.

By day the shepherd took his flocks up on to the downs, bringing them back to the arable land at night. Each night the hurdles would be in a different place so that the whole field was manured.

All across the Plain shepherds would prepare for lambing at the end of the year. Building the pens was a major operation; most were sited on the high ground away from the wet. Around Imber lambing began in January or February, though Shep Bundy remembers lambing at Christmas.

Shep was born in 1908 and began shepherding in Downton around 1927. In his ninetieth year he clearly remembered standing on the down with his father and listening to the church bells ring in Christmas. The shepherd's was a hard life, out in the open in all weathers, but for him and his contemporaries it was the sheep and not their own comfort that mattered. Shep had a shepherd's hut up on the Plain, with a cot and a fire, but there were nights when he scarcely saw it. Although he was an employee, where the sheep were concerned his word was law; woe betide the farmer who thought he knew better than his shepherd.

As for the solitary life of the shepherd, the Wiltshire dialect poet Will Meade wrote:

Here on the Plain I bide
Mindin' my sheep,
O'd Rover watches 'em
When I'm asleep.
Lonely? Lar no! Not I,
How can I be
When on the Plain I got
Good Company?

Look at the chatterin'
Starlings an' jacks,
Takin' free ride about
On the sheeps' backs.
Vightin' an' sqabblin' a bit
Now an' then,
But zoon make it up like
Christian men.

Look at thic peewit ther'
Floppin' about!
Her be afeared, 'cause her
Nest's hereabouts.
Pertendin' her wing be broke,
Artful o'd thing!
Walk on a bit – you'll zee
That cures her wing.

Then there be hundreds o'
Jack Hares an' rabbits,
Zummat alike, but wi'
Different habits.
Lonely here? No, not I,
How can I be
When on our Plain be zo
Much company?

There were 800 to 900 sheep in the Imber flocks in the early twentieth century, and Jean Morrison speaks of 10,000 at a time going down to the watering holes at Bratton. As the term 'animal with the golden hoof' suggests, sheep were a major source of income on the Plain. The sheep was a self-propelled muck-spreader, provided 'new season's fat lamb'

Shearing Sidney Dean's sheep at Northside in 1919. From left to right: Silas Pearce, Harry Meaden, Albert Daniell, Enos Matthews and Harry Marsh.

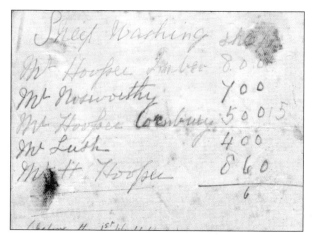

Account for washing sheep dating from before the First World War

in the spring, and wool at shearing time. The farm's shepherd would bring the flock off the Plain to be sheared. A wealthy farm might have its own team; otherwise a team would be hired. The sheep would be sheared, any nicks from the clippers dabbed with tar, and the cycle of wool production would begin again.

Travellers on the Plain

An annual pilgrimage to the sheep farms of the Plain would be made by a figure familiar to readers of Thomas Hardy: 'the reddleman'. The visits of the reddleman, like those of the tinker, brought news from near and far to many an isolated community and farmhouse. (There is a description of one such character in Peter Gurney's *Shepherd Lore* that provides another glimpse of times past.)

Cold Harbour, near Amesbury, around the turn of the century

The inn in the quiet village of Shrewton catered for travellers and their horses.

Bob Watkin's base, if he had a base, was near Devizes, and he was probably the last reddleman to ply his trade in that part of Wiltshire. Unlike a tinker with his multitude of wares, Bob had one product: reddle, though it did come in a wide variety of colours. Red was the main colour because it could easily be seen, though green, blue and black were not uncommon, and colours could be mixed to order. The preferred colour was painted on the breast of the ram before he served the ewe so the shepherd could not only tell which ewes had been served, but by which ram and when.

Wiltshire reddlemen like Bob Watkin would often have passed through Shrewton, which is surrounded by rich grazing land.

Traditionally the reddleman travelled the countryside in a small covered wagon hauled by a pony. Bob had both a wagon and a pony, and he also had a wife, all liberally tinted with reddle of various hues, but unlike others of his calling his reddle wasn't in the wagon. This was reserved for the couple's worldly goods. Instead the reddle was packed onto the backs of seven donkeys that, tied nose to tail, brought up the rear of his 'caravan'. Like those at the head of the procession, the donkeys were multi-hued as well.

Seven donkeys would have been expensive to keep, but in

Houses at Amesbury, long before the busy A303 was built

Countess Bridge, Amesbury, the location of a modern roundabout

Bob Watkin's day selling reddle was profitable. Today's flocks are measured in scores, but as we know, Jean remembers 10,000 watering in Bratton.

The reddleman covered a huge area, and on his travels he wasn't averse to a bit of poaching and judicious horse-trading, as one story illustrates. A sheep-farmer's wife asked him if he could get a donkey for her children to ride. Donkeys, though popular, weren't all that easy to get and she named a fairly high price. Bob promised to do his best, and continued on his way.

When the time came for Bob's next visit, his colourful procession turned up again but, sadly, with no donkey. As he explained to the farmer's wife, although he had tried his best, no suitable donkeys were to be had, 'Ver love nor money, ma'am.'

She told him her offer still held good and that there would be some commission for Bob if he was successful. She was obviously disappointed, so he offered to sell her one of his own donkeys. However, though they were docile and ideal for the job, they were unkempt and covered in reddle. Promising to do his best for the farmer's wife, Bob went on his way.

A short way from the village he stopped and examined his donkeys. Then, selecting the youngest and best-looking of them, he redistributed the reddle among the other animals and began to groom the selected donkey. Over a period of days he plucked away the coloured outer coat until not a trace of reddle remained. He then kept the animal segregated both from the other donkeys and the reddle, and waited for the coat to grow again.

By the time he returned to the village, the donkey's coat shone with health. Bob named a price below the one previously mentioned, handed the animal over with no word about its origins, and the farmer's wife was delighted. Bob had a satisfied client, and no doubt made a good profit after buying a replacement donkey.

There are still sheep on the Plain today, though many of those seen there in winter come from the Welsh hills. A lot come from the military training areas in the Brecon Beacons and so effectively exchange one training area for another.

These days the Army marks out the safe sheep pens with fences and notices, though one can still see the occasional square plantation of Scots Pines on an old drovers' road, marking a stopping place. These plantations were usually near a farmhouse where a weary shepherd could get food and shelter while his dog watched the flock.

In earlier centuries sheep would travel vast distances along the pine-marked drovers' roads. Sadly, up on the Plain few of the old route markers remain, though the observant traveller will still see isolated lines of pines which seem to have no purpose, and even the occasional single tree standing alone in a barren landscape. The single trees would mark junctions on tracks: Salisbury Plain tends to be a featureless place, especially in winter. Many unwary travellers have died in the mists and snow after losing their bearings, and even locals have been known to perish just a few miles from their homes. This is part of the Plain's value to the military, as wars are rarely fought with road maps.

One particular training tale will probably ring bells with many a soldier who has done his time on the Plain. Night-training exercises are always hard, especially when there is no moon. One night a squad of men left their camp in the late evening to mount a surprise attack on a position some miles away, indicated only by a map reference. It was a wet, cold, cloudy night, they were carrying full kit, and as they neared their target they knew the 'enemy' would have lookouts posted.

After about four hours they began to get worried. With their planned route and speed, they should have reached their objective after three hours. Without stars it was impossible to get an exact fix, but after a short pause and discussion they pushed on.

Three hours later, as they crested a ridge, they saw a glimmer of light below them. At last they'd found the enemy camp. Their spirits rose; military training had won the day, and they mounted a perfect surprise attack – on the base camp they had left seven hours earlier, having walked round the Plain in a circle.

The teller of that tale, a retired senior officer who wishes to remain anonymous, is certainly not alone in having lost his bearings, though, as he says, 'If you're going to make that kind of mistake it's best do it on Salisbury Plain, where you've a good chance of surviving it.'

Places like Imber and Codford were self-sufficient, self-supporting, communities, places where families stuck together and helped their own through hard times. Farms traditionally employed large numbers of men from the village, and by employing them took on responsibilities for their families as well. One of Henry Hooper's account books lists 15 men as employed and 28 women and children as dependants.

Yet there have always been some who 'slip through the net', those without family, and those who have left their place of birth and fallen on hard times. In the nineteenth and early twentieth century, such people might ultimately find themselves in the poorhouse. According to Jean Morrison's recollections, there was a poorhouse in Salisbury, but the one for the Bratton and Imber end of the Plain was in Westbury. Forbidding places, poorhouses were the subject of many a parental threat to laggardly children.

The Poor Law allowed poor people who had a cottage to stay in it, but they had to work, and the jobs they got were the

Imber's blacksmith bonding a wheel

worst, work that none with any choice of employment would want to do.

Stone-breaking was one such task. The roads over the Plain were often little more than mud tracks, and stones were rolled into the mud to make them passable. Stones would be taken from the fields and piled by the road, ready for the stone-breaker. The Poor Law would supply him with a pair of goggles (wire mesh, not glass) to protect his eyes from flying flints, and a hammer. He would wear old working clothes, with a sack folded across his head and shoulders to keep off the rain and another to sit on. Thus equipped, he would work at least a ten-hour day, for which he would be paid one or two shillings a week and loaves of bread in accordance with the size of his family.

It wasn't just a simple matter of breaking the stones, either: they had to be the right size, and someone would come along

Threshing with a steam engine

One of Fuller's photographs of victims of the Depression

Many of the homeless were forced to take all their remaining belongings with them

with a gauge to check. If the stones would not go through, they had to be broken again. However, the stone-breaker probably thought himself more fortunate than those whose poverty consigned them to the poorhouse.

As a child, Jean Morrison heard someone talking about a cousin who went into the poorhouse. The cousin was old, had no money and nowhere to go. When she arrived at the poorhouse she was stripped of her own clothes and put in the uniform of the place. This was plain long skirt, a petticoat, a blouse, some kind of a woollen shawl, shoes and, in winter, stockings. They were forbidden to wear knickers because knickers were for the upper classes.

Growing up on the Plain

Jean Morrison's memories of childhood are based not only on her own experience, in the years after the First World War, but on her observations of others. To her, it was a way of life vastly preferable to that of children today. She says about parents:

They knew by experience what to do, and they didn't put small children into a crèche, nursery school, or pre-school group. They didn't keep them shut indoors with children their own age who couldn't teach them anything, as they do now. The children were with their mother, or with a granny, an auntie, or perhaps a cousin, depending on who was available. They went about with grown-ups and they learnt things.

When I look back, the happiest time of my childhood couldn't happen now because I was out in the countryside, close to those open downs. I had a sensible sort of mother, no very grand education but a good all-round one. She had knowledge of the countryside and would take me wherever she went.

We used to go long walks. We'd go up in the short grass where the sheep had been grazing and find wild strawberries to eat and pick mushrooms. I knew all sorts of things that one could eat. In springtime she used to send me to gather the tops of nettles to cook as spinach because she believed it was good for your blood.

Pupils of Imber School between the wars
Left to right, back row: Harold Carter, Ron Wyatt, Reg Chapman, [?] White, Stephen Chapman, Len Potter; second row: Miss Burgess from Westbury, Hilda Rebbeck, Betty Pearce, Myra Pearce, Win Rebbeck, Phyllis Daniels, Maggie Carter, Stella Chapman; front row: Cyril Nash, [?] Rebbeck, Violet Potter, Ray Wyatt, Violet Rebbeck, Mary Pearce, [?] White, Dorothy Rebbeck, Douglas Chapman.

Before she started school Jean had learnt to snare a rabbit and kill it, and why flour was mixed in different ways for scones and a fruitcake. She was told the legends and stories of the Plain at her father's knee: how the West Country had traded with France throughout the Napoleonic Wars, when imported brandy, lace and other luxuries were apparently paid for in West of England woollen cloth. It was even said that Napoleon's army fought in uniforms made from that cloth. There always was smuggling across the Plain, if not within living memory, certainly in her great-grandparents' time. The story of Wiltshire's Moonrakers may be just that: a story, but hiding things from the Revenue Men used to be a way of life.

Then there were the country cures, the knowledge of the simple medicines the old women of the village passed down from generation to generation. Some things everyone knew, like eating plenty of greens in early spring. As Jean recollects:

I don't know why it worked, but it did. They used quite a lot of things which we now know have definite effects on your health. And of course, as there was no drug scare going around like now; you could go into a chemist and buy six-pennyworth of opium to relieve your really bad rheumatism.

A great-grandfather of hers who suffered a lot of pain was told by his doctor that a little opium would ease it. He lived to be over ninety and was still taking small doses to the end.

There was usually one woman in the village, often the midwife (who would sometimes arrange for the better-off to lend the less well-off baby things, or pay for medical care)

Jean Morrison

and project it to somebody else without losing control of that bit. You may know if they are ill or in need of help. You may just be putting an idea into their mind, and then you pull back that bit that you sent out and it locks into your head. . . . I've no idea how it works. I only know it does. It runs in families. I had an aunt who had it, and a great-aunt, and a great-great-aunt.

For the well-off in Imber, there were tennis parties on the courts at Seagram's, Brown's, Tinker's and Imber Court. One tournament Mollie Dean organized had 70 players and Jack Dean ferried the players from one end of the village to the other in his father's car.

Then there were the shooting parties of ten or twelve 'guns', which would be followed by cards in the evening. The party usually broke up around midnight, when the guns took some hares, partridges or pheasants home with them. The remainder would be taken to Broadhursts in Bath and sold.

Dances at Warminster, Frome, Trowbridge and Salisbury were another diversion, often going on until breakfast was served around 5 a.m. After one particular dance, one of the Deans arrived in his evening suit to help with the milking.

But the lines dividing 'upstairs' and 'downstairs' were blurring, as Jean Morrison remembers:

When I was taken out by old Mr Dyer the coachman, he always addressed me as Miss Haynes, he wouldn't have dreamt of calling me Miss Jean, or Jean. I was Miss Haynes, and my younger sister was Miss Pauline Haynes. Cousins were always Cousin Violet, or Cousin John, never just Violet or John. It was still very Victorian and Edwardian, and when I was driven round the village, or into Salisbury, all the village children curtseyed as I passed.

It was something that made Jean very uncomfortable.

Middle-class women were starting to work, at home and in the professions. Those lower down the social scale had always worked. Jean remembers when she was about three, which would have been in 1915, a farmer harnessing his wife to a plough. The couple had a smallholding and lived off what they grew and the chickens laid:

was a fund of valuable knowledge. For example, tea made from raspberry leaves eased childbirth, as well as helping with 'other female things that turn up at intervals'. She sold herbs she had gathered and dried, and knew which would cause a miscarriage when there was an illegitimate pregnancy. Cats could apparently read her thoughts and did her bidding. Of such powers, Jean says:

It's a cross between real knowledge and bit of – well, they called it witchcraft then. Now you go to a psychologist and get much worse advice. . . . It's an ability to take something out of your brain

That's the sort of hard work that women did, if they had to. She was a nice woman, one of those white faces with coarse ginger hair, and she always wore a flat cap, a man's flat cap, not a woman's one at all. But she had ankle-length skirts, no nonsense about trousers!

Of the suffragette movement, she comments: 'All the well-to-do women were furious as soon as it really took hold, because it encouraged women to break free from housework and meant they hadn't any servants. It was a disaster.' Jean has a letter, written in about 1927, from her Great-Aunt Jane to her mother in which she complains that her personal maid has just left to get married and she can't find another. She complains that they all want more than £20 a year.

Jean's generation was the first one at her social level to be brought up without staff. Her husband was fifteen years older than she was and his mother wouldn't have dreamt of bringing up two children without help. Although she didn't

Shops in Amesbury, 1930s

Imber celebrates the coronation of George V

live in a very big house, she had a full-time nursemaid. She also had a full-time maid in the kitchen, assisted by a part-time maid, and a part-time gardener.

If the First World War and suffragette movement had begun a social change, the Second World War would finish it. In the village of Imber, purchased (except for the church) by the Army in 1927, life continued largely unchanged, with occasional festive days to break the routine, such as 6 May 1935, the Silver Jubilee of George V and Queen Mary.

Imber had a good record for celebrating royal occasions and the planning was, as always, meticulous. The great barn was once again pressed into service and the event was cele-brated with Jubilee Sports at Imber Court, including an 'Egg and Spoon Handicap for Ladies over Thirty', for which the first prize was '1 lb of Ceylon Tea presented by Everetts Stores, Warminster'. No doubt the food was as generous as in 1887, when around 360 people dined in the barn on 334 lbs of meat (cold beef and mutton), 30 hot plum puddings, 20 gallons of bread and 72 gallons of ale to celebrate Queen Victoria's Golden Jubilee.

The committee was to convene a few years later for the coronation of George VI and Queen Elizabeth. Unbeknown to any at the time, it would the last celebration of its kind that Imber would see.

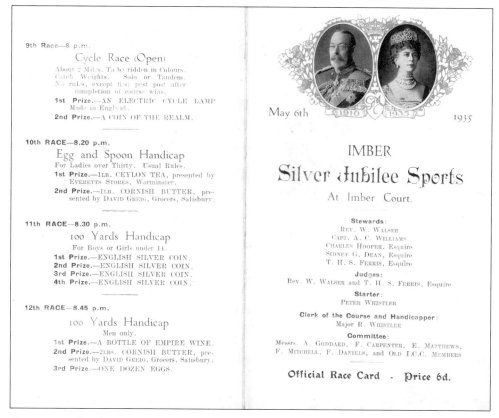

Programme for the Silver Jubilee Sports at Imber Court

Brewers and Draymen

Villages often brewed their own ale for both celebrations and everyday use, but as a county, Wiltshire has never been short of larger brewers. One of the most famous was founded in 1875, when Henry Wadworth bought the old Northgate Brewery in Devizes. Ten years later, having outgrown its

Henry Wadworth

original site, the company, with Henry Wadworth now in partnership with his brother-in-law and life-long friend John Bartholomew, moved to a purpose-built tower brewery 100 yards away. There the Wadworth Brewery sank its roots.

It is still there today, with the Bartholomew family still at the helm, and some of Henry's original equipment and the traditional methods continue to be used. With its oak casks and horse-drawn drays, the brewery retains an 'old-world' charm, but behind the image is solid financial reasoning.

Take the wooden barrels, for example. As Alastair Simms, Wadworth's cooper, says, 'Landlords view wood as being more breakable than metal. Actually a metal keg damages more easily and then has to be sent away for repair, whereas a damaged oak cask can be back in use within 24 hours.' Beer may not, offically, taste any different when drawn from the wood but, as Alastair points out, 'You can tell old casks. The beer has stained half an inch into the wood, so the flavour's got to come out.'

Even when a barrel is beyond repair it is not thrown away, but cut down to make a smaller one. So some of the wood for the casks Alastair is making now could have come from barrels used by Henry Wadworth in 1875. It is an interesting thought that some vestige of flavour from ale drunk by soldiers in that 1898 march past could be in a pint pulled on the Plain today.

It is also possible that one of the shire horses delivering around Devizes is related to a horse that delivered to the Plain, but the fact that horses reproduce and lorries don't is not the reason the brewery uses them. The two pairs of shires do the work of one vehicle. The vehicle costs £38,000, a heavy horse £2,000 – and the horse will work until it's nineteen.

If those two reasons for real horsepower are not enough, the company knows to the minute just how much free television time the horses have earned. To Gordon Snook, the head drayman, caring for them is a labour of love. He was brought up around shires on what was probably the last farm in Wiltshire to work the land using living horsepower.

Before the days of the lorry, horsepower was the only way to deliver beer to the Plain, and, unsurprisingly, the Army

Wadworth's purpose-built tower brewery

Wooden beer barrels being filled at the Northgate Brewery

was an important customer. Before the First World War Wadworth became one of the first suppliers to the Army Canteen Board, later renamed the NAAFI. It was a long day for the draymen delivering on the Plain, and thirsty work, so there are many stories of Wadworth horses plodding un-hurriedly back to Devizes with the drayman fast asleep.

A brewer's dray (right) making deliveries in Devizes

Mechanization

Wadworth's brewery also employed six outriders, who made thirty to forty calls day collecting orders. In 1930 Cecil Shepherd was one such representative, having begun as an office boy with the company in 1926. The company in those days had about thirty horses on the road, helped on long deliveries by ex-Army lorries. Mechanization was gradually creeping in.

Cecil was mechanized from the beginning: 'They bought me a T-Type Ford and I went off and learnt to drive that and went on from there.'

One of the first areas he covered was the Plain, and though there never have been many pubs in the area, there were numerous village clubs like the British Legion. Trade was good too: during exercises twenty lorries would arrive at the brewery to collect beer, and that was over and above the number of deliveries made by the Wadworth vehicles.

In the early days of Cecil Shepherd's career on the Plain, the Army still relied on the horse. He remembers the beautiful grey horses of the Scots Greys at Tidworth. He also recalls the huge Royal Army Ordnance Corps Depot at Tidworth and lots of drinking in the sergeants' mess: 'Everybody used to seem to drink all day long there, and nobody seemed to worry about it.'

He met other reps who had their stories too, like one of his predecessors who used to cycle to Tidworth to get his orders. In those days there was a little thatched pub there called The Ram and on one occasion he couldn't get inside because it was full of the Irish navvies who were building the barracks. Another of Cecil's predecessors was Tom Dickinson, who travelled the Plain on horseback.

Cecil and his colleagues visited the Tidworth Searchlight Tattoo every year. They used to pile on to the back of a lorry, go to the polo ground, and watch the searchlights pick out an

Mechanical horsepower brought its own hazards. This accident at Airman's Cross was attended by mechanics from an early AA-authorized garage as well as the police.

Salisbury Plain Motors, High Street, Amesbury

Inside Salisbury Plain Motors, which was owned by Andrew Sloane

Foden steam lorry photographed by Fuller in 1936

aircraft from Netheravon as it passed overhead. Little did they know how soon those skills were to be used in earnest over Britain's cities.

The Postal Service

Life throughout Wiltshire was changing. Lorries were replacing the horse and cart, and cars and buses the buggy and horse-drawn carriage. New businesses grew to service, sell petrol to, rescue and repair the new horseless carriage. But across the Plain, some things – including the mail – were still delivered in the old way: by cart, on horseback and very often on foot.

The 1859 Post Office Directory lists 13 commercial residents in Imber, one of whom was John Staples, shopkeeper and blacksmith. He and his wife Anne lived in Imber's oldest cottage and one of Betty Hooper's old photographs shows her sitting outside it. She remained as shopkeeper after her husband's death in 1888. Sadly, the cottage burnt down during the First World War.

According to the directory, letters to and from Imber went through Heytesbury, which was also the nearest money-order office. Edward Parker, the postman, would bring the mail over by bicycle from Codford to Chitterne, then on foot to Imber, where he had a tin hut. He used to stay in the village all day, doing odd jobs, and take the afternoon mail

Anne (Granny) Staples sitting outside her cottage

with him on his return to Codford. Alice Sparey, who took over the round in 1916, used to walk the whole way. She continued as Codford's postwoman until 1969, and died in 1973.

Imber got its own post office in 1909. Charles White's daughter Ellen Carter was the first and only postmistress, as the office closed on 17 December 1943, when the village was evacuated.

In 1939 an article in the *Post Office Magazine* was headed: 'The loneliest Post Office in England – Imber, Wiltshire.' Its

Alice Sparey, who delivered Codford's post – on foot – from 1916 to 1969, outside her cottage in 'Frog Alley' (its real name was Doughty's Lane)

Codford Post Office

'The loneliest Post Office in England – Imber, Wiltshire'
(Post Office Magazine, 1939)

author spoke of seeing 'no cottages, no farms, only sheep and the illimitable skyline of the Plain' on the journey to Imber. The surrounding countryside was, according to the article, 'a clean sweet peaceful land – with only one disturbing feature. On the downs were tracks of Army tanks.' Imber was described as 'quiet, but every Thursday an omnibus does pass through on its way to Devizes!'

Sadly, this tranquillity was due to end all too soon.

FIVE

War Again: 1939–45

Codford and Imber in the Second World War

Between the wars life in Codford, as in Imber, continued largely unchanged though, as Harry Coles tells us, change was in the air:

Up till 1938 nothing much had been done in the village to alter its appearance or character. The temporary shops and other legacies of the war had been cleared away, but little or no fresh building had taken place, although several businesses that had come temporarily to the village in the first war did stay on and found permanent premises.

The Parish Council had previously discussed housing, street lighting, and water supply, and in connection with water a well-attended public meeting in 1938 was warned by one worthy gentleman of the danger of providing people with water out of pipes. 'What!' he exclaimed, drawing himself up with indignation, 'They will be demanding baths next!' Added to this awful thought was the threat: 'Your rates will go up by nine shillings in the pound.' That clinched it – no water!

But houses were being built by the local authority and the first eight were erected and occupied in 1938. Oddly enough they had baths, which were regarded as a joke, as there was no provision for hot water except a small copper, and no water supply except one hand pump between the eight houses. They were not central in the village, but they were there – and they had baths! The village had started to grow.

The rumbling of tanks was now being heard at night and the Parish Council was concerned about the noise, so they decided to see what could be done about it. There was even talk of a by-pass road. Then came that fateful day in September – we were at war again!

It was with feelings of dull resentment that the village accepted the fact that another war had started. The sense of security engendered by the National Governments of the Thirties was now shown to be false, and there was a feeling that somebody, somewhere, had let us down.

But the grim situation was with us, for stabbing the darkness of the night sky were the probing pencils of light from the searchlights. An eerie feeling of danger seemed always to be with them and their restless search of the heavens. Then suddenly they would be gone, making the darkness seem much more intense.

The presence in the village of military personnel presaged the fact that troops were to be stationed here again, and it was not long before there was a Company of the Forty-Third Wessex Division R.E. in our midst. They were men from the Trowbridge and Chippenham area, and they settled in like old friends, which they soon were. Camps began to be built again, not as one might have supposed where they stood before – that would never do! No, fresh sites had to be found, in some cases adjacent to former sites and, in others, entirely new.

The main difference from the First World War was that there was not the same upheaval in the daily life of the village. The construction work went on at a faster pace. Transport was not a problem, the roads were better, mechanical aids were available, and the contractors brought the men to the sites and took them away again. There were no temporary shops or odd buildings set up. The huts for the troops had not so much to be built as assembled, and almost without notice the camps were there – not so many or so widespread as before, so they caused less interference with the business of the farming fraternity, for which they were duly thankful.

With the outbreak of war practically all social and other activities came to a stop, except for the Women's Institute, which carried on, war or no war! They celebrated their twenty-first anniversary in 1945 in the Congregational Church Room. In other ways the village soon became aware of the situation: rationing, the call-up of all the eligible young men, and the severe shortage of petrol. The blackout regulations were a source of worry to police, wardens and villagers alike, and getting around at night with so

The Codford Home Guard marches through the village

little illumination was a nightmare, especially where livestock had to be dealt with. We were also getting to know 'Lord Haw Haw' – 'This is Jarmany calling' – with his nightly radio broadcast of British disasters. He might have had more effect had it no been for Sir Winston Churchill, who unfailingly cut him down to size! Even so, the situation was grim.

The return of men from Dunkirk reminded us that the war was actually getting closer, and every able-bodied man and woman was enrolled for some job in case the need arose. As well, we had the Wardens' Home Guard, and Women's Voluntary Service. We had no arms of course, but heavy old farm carts and implements were looked out to provide roadblocks. It was believed that the invasion would be some time in September 1940. So the river was dredged to make it impassable for tanks, and pillboxes were set up at strategic points.

We waited, and nothing happened. Autumn drew on to Winter, the bombing of big cities continued – we were not, it seemed, to be called up for any defence. We were relieved but not relaxed, as the bombers passed high overhead and were caught in the silver swordpoints of the searchlights, for we knew of death and destruction being carried to towns and cities of our own land.

Evacuees arrived unexpectedly after several false reports of their coming had been circulated, and the business of finding people willing to billet them was a headache. The truth of the saying 'An Englishman's home is his castle' was brought home to us. Arrangements for the evacuees were very poorly organized. Plans there might have been, but there was not anything like the preparations necessary for such an emergency, added to which, much of the available accommodation had been taken up by relatives and friends of men stationed in the village. Where room was available, there was often nothing in the way of equipment, so this had to be borrowed. For some reason everybody seemed to want girls, not boys! The number we had to deal with was not large, and eventually all were accommodated somewhere.

To have said that the evacuees were happy would be untrue – everything was against them, all was so different. The darkness frightened them, their husbands and fathers were in London, and many soon returned to their homes. A few remained and were quite happily absorbed into the village and its life. In addition, a preparatory school for boys, complete with staff, came from Bognor to Ashton Gifford House in 1940. They too, did not leave and became the well-known preparatory school 'Greenways'.

This was a different war from the first one, not so much man to man, but machine against machine. Our Air Raid Wardens did their nightly patrols; our other services were well manned but not required, for with so many military personnel in the village there was little need for them. Although there were a few incidents from enemy action in the Parish, no damage to life or property occurred. Bombs were dropped close enough to shake the houses, but nothing worse.

It was the Sixth Armoured Guards Brigade who now occupied the camps. They were a fine body of men, and probably the most popular troops to have been in the village during either war.

Among the officers who arrived with the Brigade was Tony Hayward, now a retired Brigadier who still lives just south of the Plain. He was the liaison officer at the time and remembers there being 200 tanks in Codford. Many were driven by trainee drivers and a fair numbers of walls, and even a few cottages, suffered during that period. Tanks were new to the Guards, and some were more mechanically inclined than others. The Brigadier recollects one such officer who commanded the 4th Battalion. He was:

a marvellous man known as Bushy Shrub Tree. He wasn't very mechanically minded and when we turned to into armour I don't think he really understood it. He is reputed to have once said 'Stop, stop, it'll unscrew!' when he saw the chap testing the power traverse on his turret and turning it round and round.

But training on the Plain can be just as deadly as the battlefield, as can demonstrations, as the Brigadier witnessed in April 1942. The demonstration was to be a dress rehearsal for a visit by Winston Churchill the following day, when he was to be shown the ground-attack capabilities of the new ten-gun Hurricane fighter. Some wooden silhouettes of soldiers had been set up as targets about 500 yards from the VIP viewing area. The Brigadier now takes up the story:

I was there with Sir Maurice Bruce, who is now Lord Abedare, and we were standing watching this thing. The first two or three planes came over and shot up the targets, then the fourth plane seemed to be wavering a bit, it wasn't quite sure which way. . . . So I said, 'Maurice, I think he's going to shoot at us,' and he said, 'Oh, don't be absurd, Tony.' But sure enough, he did.

An old Home Guard Colonel was shot right beside them and reports that trickled out later spoke of 27 killed and 68 others seriously wounded. As the Brigadier remarked, 'It proved the efficiency of the ten-gun Hurricane, but in a rather unfortunate way.'

The story goes that when Churchill was due to visit he was sent a signal explaining what had happened, to which he replied, 'I'm not frightened. Are you?'

In 1943, as Harry Coles tells us, the Americans arrived:

and what a contrast this was. Their enormous transport vehicles with teams of drivers, and the mechanization of everything to do with the war was, for us, an education in modern methods of warfare.

Somehow, they never looked like soldiers, and certainly many of them, it seemed, had never wanted to be. Those that came here were mostly from the country places, quiet towns, homesteads and farms. Softly spoken, happy, kindly natured men, who missed their homes and loved to sit in the houses of the village people, smoke their endless American cigarettes and cigars, and just talk of their Pops and Moms. Delightful companions, they were just as we had met them in books, and brought home to us the fact that all Americans do not come from New York, or are Chicago gangsters. They made many friends, and we were impressed by the fact that they were proud of their British ancestry – if they had any. What a party they gave our schoolchildren at Christmas, for they, at any rate, had no rationing problems!

A large American Club was set up for their use in the Wool Stores, and it was during their stay that a visiting Ensa company, which included Gracie Fields, gave a performance in the large repair depot in the paddock of Manor House. They left in 1944 and were replaced by another batch. These were as different as chalk from cheese. Most of them appeared to have come from large

The Codford Milk Bar was a popular meeting-place for local residents of all ages and for the American soldiers who arrived during the war.

cities. Their numbers were not great, as the war was at last drawing to a close, so they were not with us for long.

But they were there long enough to need to train, and their training meant the end of the village of Imber. In 1943 every household in the village got a notice to quit from the War Department. Betty Hooper recalls that the letters were brought round one morning by a man who returned later in the day to collect them all again, but one of the villagers had put his in his pocket and gone out for the day. Thanks to him, and Betty's detective work, that letter still exists.

Many ex-residents believe the letters were collected again because they promised the residents that they would be able eventually to go back to Imber. The sentence in question comes towards the end of the letter and reads:

if you are so unfortunate as not be able to find alternative accommodation, and it is necessary to remove your furniture to store, the [War] Department will refund the cost of removal to store and reasonable storage until you can find another house, or until the Imber area is again open for occupation, whichever is the earlier.

Copy of the eviction notice sent to every household in Imber in 1943

The tenants had only a matter of weeks in which to pack up and leave, and there was all the stock to sell, not to mention their machinery. The first sale was held at Seagram's, Brown's, and Quebeck farms on Saturday, 11 December. The second sale was at Edington on Wednesday, 15 December, two days before the village had to be cleared. In all 5,200 sheep and 70 head of 'choice dairy cattle' were sold, along with implements and machinery. The fact that so many sheep were on the market inevitably the lowered the price, but sold they were, and Imber emptied on time.

However, such was their certainty that they would return that some people left possessions behind, and villagers say the Americans treated their homes with respect and did little or no damage at all. It was the British Army, they believe, that caused the damage when they moved into Imber. Whoever was responsible, enormous damage was certainly done early on, and the wind and rain have played their part in returning the village to the Plain from which many of its buildings were made.

The Americans weren't the only foreign visitors to the Plain. There were the Polish volunteers, various nationalities of refugee, and of course the POWs in the various camps.

Men away from home also attract another sort of visitor, one of whom was unexpectedly encountered by Ron Sutton when he was cutting hay. He was using a hay knife and,

As I started to cut the hay out I couldn't get the knife down there. I thought, what's here? I've got a fox or some rabbits or something down there.

I pulled the hay back and was surprised to find a woman in there. She was a prostitute who'd escaped from a hospital in Bristol or somewhere. She had one of her legs in plaster and luckily for her I'd put the knife across the one with plaster on it.

She was all covered up in this hole, and she stank. There were packets of fags, and she'd been messing about with the Eytie prisoners. There were Italian POWs about and she'd been doing her duty with them.

We used to call them Haystack Annies. They used to go up by the dump where they entertained the troops. There was Haystack Annies up over the top there. The troops and all that used to go up there. You could see them queuing up all over the road. From all over the place they came, and the Yanks used to put them up somewhere.

Ron Sutton was born in 1921 and, at the time of writing, still lives in the small cottage he was born in. His father was

Canadian kitbags arriving at Larkhill

a Canadian and came to Codford as a soldier in the First World War. Ron was brought up during the Depression and remembers his mother scrubbing floors for 6d an hour. He also remembers how she went without food so that the rest of the family could eat. The generation who lived through such times knew the value of a job, which may be why Ron's first job lasted for thirteen and a half years and his second for thirty-six.

SIX

The Postwar Years

The Army

Finally the war was over and Salisbury Plain began to settle down again. Soldiers, POWs and refugees could return home if they wished, though several liked the Plain and stayed. It was only to Imber that no one returned, although the villagers still confidently expected to.

Of course the Army was still there, changed from a wartime to a peacetime force, and peopled with that often reluctant breed of soldier, the National Serviceman.

The Army's second fifty years on the Plain would see huge changes, though their effects would not seem as great to those who lived there. Weapons would change as warfare itself changed. Mechanized units needed more space, especially when they lost the training areas in Germany. Shells needed to travel further to be tested, and complex exercises involving all three services became more frequent. However, one of the biggest changes for many was the Army's view of the Plain itself.

There are those serving who can remember ancient tumuli being used as tank traps, but the Army's watchword now is conservation. 'No entry' signs guard sites of ancient villages and young plantations of trees. Those who plan the battles now consider nature's needs as much as their own, and groups of conservationists spend their spare time re-introducing barn owls in impact zones and other wild stretches of the Plain.

David Saul is Defence Land Agent for Wessex and the South West and one of his tasks is to ensure that the military are good neighbours as well as good landlords. He is also responsible for ensuring the public's right of access. As he says:

MOD policy, where it's compatible with military training, is to encourage public access, and there are over 270 miles of public rights of way on Salisbury Plain alone. So we encourage and actually manage public rights on the training area. There are parts of it where it is dangerous for people to go – they're clearly signed – and there are parts where they are welcome to go.

What of the changes the Army has made? David Saul again:

Originally we believe it was all forested, and the trees would have been cleared by people developing the land for agriculture many thousands of years ago.

If you imagine the arable farming when the MOD bought the land, quite sizeable bits were under the plough and were being farmed for corn, and that was put back to grass as part of the MOD acquisition. And that MOD ownership of it of course has kept it as rolling grassland and that's maintained the conservation value of the site enormously.

As for the Plain itself, to him: 'There's an openness about the place. It has almost a magical quality. It's inherently beautiful and it has that wild empty feel that's perhaps rather like a moorland that you find in the middle of southern England.'

David Saul's feelings are common among those whose job it is to look after the Salisbury Plain Training Area, and no look at the Plain today would be complete without a word from its current Commandant, Lt.-Col. Mike Jelf. For him, the military side tends to be the easiest part, partly, as he says, because he's had a little practice. What can be more difficult is understanding how important archaeology is, and the conservation issues that go with it. But the military do recognize that the archaeology, once destroyed, will never come back.

About the issue of pollution, Lt.-Col. Jelf comments:

The damage we do to the environment in terms of pollution is obviously of great importance. We are in danger of creating pollution by leakages and spillages, and we have in place measures to limit that. But in terms of the flora and fauna, they do grow back, but at the same time we've got to make sure we fully understand what those issues are and not dismiss them as unimportant while we conduct our training. Though at the end of the day, I'm afraid to say, training is priority number one here on the Plain.

We have big vehicles like Challenger and Warrior that rip up the countryside, and we've got AS90, the super gun as some people have called it, which makes an awful lot of noise. We have helicopters, we throw mud onto the road, and all these things we have to deal with.

But training has to continue. This is our best training area. It's the only training area where we can have fair freedom of movement, avoid stereotype range work, and do armoured exercises with a relatively free amount of movement. We can have a brigade-level exercise here, with two thousand troops and a few hundred vehicles, many of them tanks, and Warrior armed fighting vehicles, so there are a lot of issues that we have to be aware of.

Asked whether there will ever be a time when the Army leaves Salisbury Plain, he replies:

It will be the day when we don't have an Army, frankly. And I think there would be an awful lot of support for us retaining Salisbury Plain from people like English Nature and English Heritage.

Why is Stonehenge so tightly protected now? I remember when I first went to Stonehenge when I was nine years old, you could walk up and touch the stones. You can't do that now, except in special circumstances, because the tramping of thousands of feet

Camouflaged AS90s

'The enemy' waits to mount a surprise attack.

over dozens and dozens of years wears away the ground. There are certain parts of this training area which, by nature of being a military training area, are protected for generations to come, and we recognize that and have protective measures. But it would be awfully difficult if the general public was at liberty to roam wherever it wanted to. It would effect the archaeology and it would certainly effect the conservation side.

What would happen to the stone curlew? We already have problems with people trying to take photographs of it and perhaps remove stone curlews' eggs. It is an extremely rare bird, and where they're breeding is quite sensitive information, because the only way we're going to have any success is to leave them alone and provide the sort of environment that they can breed in.

Then of course there are the farmers who work the land the military own. With the military as their landlords they tend to be circumspect in their comments. They naturally take a dim view of tanks ploughing across a field sown with crops, or pieces of military ordnance going astray (one farmer opened his front door to find a smoking shell on the porch).

Mistakes are occasionally made, but these days the impression is of military and civilian life existing side by side fairly peaceably, which has not always been the case over the last century.

Has technology made the modern Army soft? Bouncing across the Plain in half a million pounds' worth of Warrior

Camouflaged armour hidden in the shadows of a wood at sunset

Armoured Infantry Fighting Unit (AIFV), or two and a half millions pounds' worth of Challenger Tank, might be better than walking, but it's no Sunday-afternoon run in the country.

Technology has brought about changes. In some exercises laser beams now simulate bullets to tell both men and machine when they've been hit. There has also been a move towards computerized simulators, some of which may well save wear on the Plain, although nothing can replace the noise and confusion of running battles, helicopter attacks and living out on the Plain for days on end. Such exercises can be fun and, as a senior officer said, following one particularly muddy, cold, and misty three-day jaunt across the Plain, 'Training has to be fun.'

This feeling is not restricted to the officers and planners, either. At the end of 24 hours of non-stop 'fighting', one soldier was asked what the best thing about the exercise was. 'Not having to wash,' he replied with a grin, his face caked in mud and both hands wrapped firmly round a mug of tea.

Not washing may be one attraction to life in the open, but sunset in a wood, with camouflaged armour hidden among the shadows, can be a magical experience. Soldiers, like shepherds, share the Plain with foxes, badgers, rabbits and hares. Col. Mark Jackson, Commander Battle Group Training Unit remarked, 'Today's soldiers are a lot Greener than they used to be' (something Lt.-Col. Jelf would no doubt be delighted to hear).

The villagers

Following the Second World War, modernization set in in the villages with a vengeance. In most houses, electricity was installed, and running water. Candles were now kept for emergencies and the tea-strainer was used only for straining tea, not fishing out silverfish from the water gathered from a nearby stream.

Eventually mains drainage would link house with house and village with village, for most people at least, something that Jean Morrison, for one, views as a shocking waste. She has a septic tank, as well as a network of pipes that can recycle water and domestic waste back into the earth from whence it came.

Codford changed in the same way as other villages and, as Harry Cole describes, running water arrived there too, in its own good time.

Off licence, Codford, in 1949

The first postwar council houses were now ready for occupation, and out of a host of applicants the Council made their recommendations. The houses had water laid on which was connected to the supply installed by the Military Authorities. This led to a demand by other residents for a water supply, and this demand was implemented when it was discovered that one place other than a council house had been connected to the supply. It happened to be the off-licence premises, and one was prompted to ask if the proprietor knew the story of his well and was nervous over what might come up in the next bucketful.

Some years earlier, in the days of a previous licensee, friends used to foregather in the back kitchen for a quiet little booze. Late one evening, Charlie joined a few pals there, after he had been down to the eel stage and come away with some good eels, which he left in a bag on the well-cover before joining his friends inside. Later, steamed up with good warmed cider and ginger, he picked up his bag and wended his way homewards, but on arriving there, he made the unhappy discovery that there was a hole in the bottom of the bag, and some of the eels were gone. The one thing not done in cases of this sort was to make enquiries – you were sure to hear if any eels had been seen in the street! – but no such news was forthcoming. Gone down a drain, thought Charlie.

Months later, when the bucket was drawn up from the well, there was a fine fat eel in it. Here was a mystery. How had eels got into a 60-foot well? Charlie might have enlightened them, for while he was inside enjoying the convivial company, the eels had squeezed through a hole in the bag, and slithered under the ill-fitting well-cover down into the water – a very fishy business altogether!

The Rural District Council eventually took over the water supply from the War Department, and by 1951 piped water was available for anyone who wanted it, but not without some grumbling about the cost of having it installed.

Not long after the arrival of the water, Codford joined in the country's sadness at the death of George VI and then, as Harry Cole relates, threw itself into the excitement of the forthcoming Coronation:

The Coronation of Queen Elizabeth II now occupied our attention and arrangements were made for a day of general rejoicing. Nobody living had any experience of a queen's coronation, and as she was young it would probably be the last English coronation of which many people would have any knowledge, English queens having a habit of reigning for a long time. It must be a day to remember, so our energies were devoted to that end. All seemed well and the day was awaited with keen anticipation. Alas, the weather did not play its part, and although we were much more fortunate than many other places, the afternoon was dull and wet. The procession went well, and had just finished when the rain came down. The evening was finer, and a huge bonfire had been built on Codford Circle, which is the highest point in this area. From the top could be counted a dozen or more bonfires, and this fine sight transported us back to the days of the first Queen Elizabeth and the Armada – or so it seemed – so we were compensated for our damp day!

The fortunate people who had television sets were besieged by friends and neighbours. For the first time in history, millions of people were able to see the actual coronation ceremony, and hear the inspiring music and singing which was part of it. Truly a wonderful experience.

By 1954 television aerials were a much more common feature of the village and there was no doubt the attraction it had for the village people. It had enormous advantage of being visual. It entailed no journeys out of doors; it cost no more on H.P. than was previously spent on the cinema. What was more important, there were grandstand viewpoints of racing, cricket, football, athletics and current events. Television widened our experience of plays and enabled us to set standards of performance. It was obviously going to be a serious competitor to local interests and events.

Sadly, the arrival of television saw the weekly cinema close at Codford Club and whist-drive attendances decline. 'Civilization' had arrived. In 1960 the railway station closed too, with villagers happily relying on buses and their own cars. But, in 1962, as the people of Codford filled kettles from their taps to make a cup of tea and perhaps considered where to drive to the next day, Salisbury Plain reminded them where they lived. Harry Cole writes:

The great snowstorm of 1962 was a repeat performance of 1927, and the onset of the blizzard occurred approximately at the same time but in severity it was worse than in 1927. It persisted for some days with little or much snowfall and by 1 January 1963 the roads were almost impassable. Mechanical methods were used to clear roads enough to allow limited use, but the blizzard was followed by frost and the work of clearing slowed up. Although the countryside was very beautiful, a lot of sheep were lost.

This is how Harry Cole, writing in 1964, summarized the changes wrought on his village in the previous half-century:

The last fifty years has been an amazing time. Ours has been a great age of history, perhaps the greatest that the world has ever known. So much that is momentous has occurred. It has not always been a happy time, but certainly a very interesting and

The last train ever to stop at Codford, on 17 September 1955: the 17:20 Salisbury to Cardiff train, pulled by 5080 and 4968. Nine passengers got off. The signalman was Mr J. Morgan.

exciting one! Mr Churchill once said that to change was to progress, and can there have been more changes in the short space of fifty years? They have come about gradually and in tune with the trend over the whole country.

One result of this is to make us more like town-dwellers. We have become more cosmopolitan in type and character, which may be a good thing, but we have less sense of belonging to the place than used to be the case. 'You must preserve the people of a place if you want to preserve its character.' We are courteous to each other, with the politeness that is natural to the countryman, but we do not always know those whose greeting we acknowledge. We are in a sense strangers to each other – our interests are not entered or in common as was formerly the case when the only occupation was farming or work connected with it. We seem to have become moulded to a common pattern and have less individuality.

Fifty years ago there were a number of characters who though often unlettered, possessed a natural culture and store of knowledge. Snakeshole Jack – why 'Snakeshole' is not clear, but he did have a wide knowledge of edible fungi and where they could be found – claimed to be able to find truffles and it is on record that a very large one of over 4 lbs was dug up on Boyton Park. He was a jovial, talkative old fellow and he certainly knew where to find mushrooms in a bad year, and morels (which seemed to disappear when he died). Perhaps only he knew where they grew. Black Jimmy, who lived a hermit's life in the middle of the grove, was another. The children were frightened of him and his wild appearance and black whiskers. He occasionally emerged to go to the shop but he did not encourage visitors to his hide-out. He was said to have come from a good family and he was well spoken and knew the habits of birds and wildlife intimately. It is a fact that since his removal the nightingales, which used to be heard frequently, are now heard but rarely.

Farming methods have been revolutionized and the status of the farm worker has risen. The ploughman with his team against the skyline is there no longer. The shepherds who tended large flocks of Hampshire Down Sheep in the locality are now few. The sheep bells are mostly silent. Haymaking and harvesting have lost their colourful significance and excitement. You cannot enthuse over a hay baler or combine harvester, invaluable though they are in tricky weather; the rick yard has ceased to exist, the water meadows have gone and the drowner no longer drowns anything. Nor does the clang of the anvil bring the children coming home from school to the blacksmith's open door. There is a blacksmith but he comes in a motor van from eleven miles away to shoe the hunters and ponies.

Farming has become big business for the scientist and economist with enormous capital invested in machinery and labour-saving devices.

Livestock farming tends to assume the aspect of a production line; new feeding methods shorten the life of nearly all our farm animals, they walk in as calves at one door and out of the other as baby beef at ten months; ewes more prolific; pigs up to bacon weight at five and a half months; chicken by the million; hens in batteries, heavier crops of corn; milking parlours for cows with the milk handled by machines from cow to consumer; the stepping up of milk yields; artificial insemination; wider veterinary knowledge and practice; antibiotics; injections; elimination of TB and other diseases; the overall urgency to speed things up; earlier maturity,

quicker growth, larger crops – these are the slogans of our farming practice. There is no time to stand and stare.

Perhaps the greatest transformation of the last fifty years is in the matter of women's dress. What would have happened in 1914 if a young woman had dared to walk down the street in shorts and a brassière? She would have been arrested! Nowadays in the summer-time – but that's another story!

But generally clothes are lighter, and more colourful, and although less durable perhaps and much less voluminous, they make our village women and girls more attractive. Their long hair has gone or nearly so, and there is a freedom of movement which is certainly more healthy. The children too wear more colourful clothes and less of them. Fewer hats are worn by the girls and with their short hair and slacks they often look like boys. Men's clothes have not changed so much; lighter materials, easier to get about in, but otherwise much the same. Oddly, whiskers are coming back and long-haired young men with sideboards – well, well!

In the educational field many changes have taken place. Our children no longer stay at the village school until they are old enough to leave and go to work. They pass from Primary to Junior and from there to Senior or Grammar Schools. The extended school-leaving age has given more opportunities for advanced education for many promising pupils from the village. One such has indeed become an Oxford don in her special field, one a doctor and one a hospital matron. Whether this wider education has led to an earlier mental maturity on the part of our children is certainly debateable but that they are physically mature at an earlier age seems undeniable. What is very uncertain is whether they are as emotionally mature or secure at this earlier age – they often seem perplexed and frustrated by the complexities of modern living.

Political allegiance, once seen in strong expression on the part of supporters, is now no longer such a feature at elections. Most of us do not trouble to attend meetings; we get our information, if that is what it can be called, from the turgid headlines of the brash dailies, or from television appearances by our would-be leaders, and there seems an absence of clear-cut issues.

Our housing situation is very different. Since 1928 nearly 100 houses of one sort or another have been added to the village. Seventy of these are Council houses which have been built in the last 25 years. Many older cottages have been modernized and brought up to date with modern conveniences. Housewives now have houses with bathrooms, electric light and power, running water, sanitation and labour-saving appliances. The drudgery of household chores has largely gone and many wives regularly go to employment in neighbouring towns, as do many of the menfolk, and there is still an unsatisfied demand for houses.

In matters medical, we are now enjoying a very different service from that provided in 1914. The advance of medical science, surely the greatest progress in any field in the history of the country, has revolutionized treatment for almost every known disease. We are nursed from before we are born to the time when we defy the efforts of all the specialists and shuffle off this mortal coil. We are kept fitter and active to a much later age and so able to enjoy life for many more year than formerly. All this is a reason for much satisfaction, but we do seem to consume an awful lot of nerve pills and to suffer from more neuroses – pressure on the emotions and kindred ailments. I do not think there were so many of these fifty years ago!

No longer do we take pride in our allotments; they nearly all disappeared after the last war. The village flower show, an important festival in our lives, is no longer held. The gentleman who used to walk solemnly down the main street bearing aloft his huge marrow, with name and date grown into it, has passed away. The children no longer gather wild flowers.

Our interests and amusements have not so much changed as taken on a new form. Radio and television have replaced the occasional evening concert by the glee singers. The children's entertainments of former days and singing are heard no more. Perhaps there is nothing to sing about! Our village dances are not what they were. Waltzing is an almost forgotten art, and time and tune have been replaced by what has been described as 'spasmodic evolutions of mating cormorants' and 'idiotic clamours of frenetic joy'. These are strong terms but the young people do seem to get a kick out of it, so perhaps it's not a bad thing for them to let off steam in this way. Yeah! Yeah! Yeah!

The fantastic rise in the ease of motor transport has contributed more than any other single factor to our changed habits. Distance has been annihilated and we walk very much less than we used to do. Nearly everybody goes on holiday, nearly always by car, and on Sundays off to the seaside or some place of interest. The regular attendance at church or chapel with a walk round the countryside with the family afterwards has ceased. The number of regular worshippers is low. There is respect for the Churches and their ministers but formal Christianity no longer claims our allegiance.

We seem to have become more self-centred and are concerned with the business of our own living to the exclusion of everything else. We have developed an insatiable appetite for material possessions, easy money, pools, bingo and short-cuts to affluence. The car has become our symbol of material progress. The bigger the better!

The Church is no longer the centre of our village life and if our new-found affluence has not brought all the joy and satisfaction it promised, it provides escape – but at a cost. Although there is less physical hardship, there is probably more depression and dissatisfaction.

Nevertheless the village, though it has grown, stays largely as it was. The land remains. Seed-time and harvest, Summer and Winter, Spring days of beauty and Autumn days with trees in their coloured dresses come round in their seasons. We have friends we know and love – all these things are ours in the village.

Supernatural sightings

Over recent years UFOs and crop circles have replaced the legendary Wild Hunt of the Devil, which was said to leave a black dog on Black Dog Hill in Warminster, and instead of fairy circles and the little people, the current preoccupation is with aliens and messages from other galaxies. Nevertheless, as V.S. Manley explains his book *Folk-Lore of the Warminster District*, the little people may well have a basis in fact. As he explains in the chapter 'Fairy Tree':

Many fairy tales are exaggerated or elaborate tales of the little dark race of Picts, survivors of the Stone Age, who lived in underground dwellings in remote places in the woods when later arrivals in this country displaced them from their former haunts. Shy they were, though non-aggressive, befriending their neighbours instead. Glamorgan folk are their modern representatives.

Where North Lane meets the Half below Blue Ball, Bugley, once stood a large oak tree. There, late at night, elves were sometimes seen gambolling. If a child should come upon them, they would invite him to their home beneath the tree. Inside he would see elves sitting around a table playing games whilst others were running about the table itself. After giving their visitor something to eat, they would provide him with a fairy bath. Then they would watch him to see which way he would try to get out. If he climbed upwards he would be warned of an evil spirit, and if downwards he would become an angel and never return home. After a time they would show him the proper way out, but it would be dark and he would feel giddy after his adventures, so they put him on his road again, but never would he be able to find them.

V.S. Manley also tells us that fairy rings in the grass are caused by the Champignon Fungus, not by tiny midnight dancers.

Fairies, crop circles and UFOs have fascinated residents and visitors to the Plain for many years. Jean Morrison again:

There were crop circles round here, particularly up on the top of the downs near our big white horse, long before people were talking about crop circles. We've had several since which I think are very suspicious. One I saw being formed with the aid of a rope and some young lads. But a few summers back we had a Japanese team up on the top of Brighton Cross who were watching for these circles and nothing happened, so they packed up and went. Next night there was a crop circle in the area they had been watching. A local boy rushed up when he saw what was there and told me that it was warm to touch. So what caused that I don't know.

Generations before me they would have said it was a fairy circle. When you saw one of these dust whirlwinds that you occasionally get, that was the fairies travelling invisibly within the whirlwind. So don't ask me what a crop circle is or how it's made. It's

The crop circle photographed by the Boscombe Down aircrew

either a fake or it's something queer. Mostly fakes, and they're getting fancier and fancier. They're beginning to be cut in the shapes of some of the recorded, printed, swirling circles of the early Celtic races. So somebody's got the same books I've got.

Some crop circles are certainly fakes, but many are less easily explained away. The one above, photographed by an aircrew from Boscombe Down, was created in daylight in about half an hour. The timing can be verified because the first time an aircraft passed over the site the circle wasn't there; when it returned about half an hour later, it was. Perhaps significantly, the field is just about opposite Stonehenge.

And UFOs, does Jean think they are the same kind of thing?

I've seen crop circles, though not at a time I'd seen UFOs. And I've seen these round, circular UFOs, but not at a time when there were any circles. They don't seem connected. I don't know what causes it. I don't know what these flying saucers are. I only know that they are there. They're solid. They're not anything to do with imagination, and they have a power of movement that no flying machine that I've seen could equal.

Go down to Yeovilton and you need earplugs. They've got planes that will go vertically up and down, but they're so noisy. The flying saucer is absolutely silent. Even I can't hear it, and my hearing is as good as a cat's, even now, so what is the power?

One of Jean's UFO sightings was from her own cottage. The machine hovered silently not far away and she felt it was observing her. She couldn't sense what 'it' was, only that she was being observed. It then shot thousands of feet up into the air, and finally flew out of sight. Like many people, she had been inclined to assume that UFOs were experimental military aircraft. They always seem to come from about the same place on the Plain and travel in the same direction. But their silence and style of flight puzzle her.

UFOs, crops circles, legends, ghost stories and even magic are subjects that have long since exercised the imaginations of those who have dwelt on the Plain, but none has caused as much interest as Stonehenge.

Jean used to visit the stones when she was a child. A few months ago she walked among them again for the first time in years. As she walked she touched them, as if renewing an old friendship, which indeed she was. She feels it is unlikely that the constant stream of visitors has taken away any of their power, because, after, all, some of the stones

came from Wales and some came from Avebury; they've been considered part of an ancient religion in all those centuries and centuries, whether people come or not. It doesn't make any difference. They're the equivalent of a cathedral or a temple. They're never considered to have lost anything because people visit them. They even gain as they grow older and older.

As for the stones' more recent worshippers, she remarks:

The Druids stuff is a bit of learned nonsense dating mainly from the seventeenth and eighteenth centuries, because these are far, far older than the Druids. Druids are mere newcomers compared

Jean Morrison visiting Stonehenge

with these stones. These belong to the really early Stone Age. They are contemporary with the legends that were being told in the Old Testament, where they speak of the stones that there were in Palestine. At the beginning of the Temple in the Bible, they are forbidden to use a metal tool because it was new-fangled technology, nothing to do with the ancient religion.

Those who have been lucky enough to wander among the stones and touch them may well have felt something more than their age and mystery. Jean Morrison certainly has. 'Sometimes,' she says, 'you could swear that if you turned round quickly enough you would see somebody just close to you.' She experiences this sensation not just at Stonehenge, however, but in many places, such as ancient barrows and burial grounds and near

a bit of the Plain near Brighton Castle, where we know King Alfred fought one of the decisive battles of this country. You suddenly feel if only you could just see through some invisible barrier you'd be able to see him and his men there. Perhaps they're up there in the twilight.

There will be those to whom such stories are fanciful, mere products of the imagination, out of place in a scientific age but, walking among the stones in the moonlight, little imagination is required to hear voices from the past.

Epilogue

It is sad to think that the community of Imber lost the chance to follow Codford into the future. Until the evacuation Imber had slumbered for hundreds of years in its hollow on the Plain. Even the evacuation caused little stir in the surrounding county as it was secret, Imber being referred to merely as 'a village' in the press.

Most of the villagers wanted their homes back, and did try to return in the 1960s, but it was too late. Councillor Austin Underwood from Amesbury campaigned hard to get the Army off the Imber Ranges and raised a great deal of support both locally and nationally. In June 1960 he was quoted as saying, 'Imber was murdered by wartime regulations and now the War Department are just fooling around there in this nuclear age.' (Although, as one former resident remarked not long ago, 'During the war we only lost our homes; others lost their lives.')

A mass rally was held, with press and television reports of 1,200 people thronging the narrow road across the Plain to Imber. The procession gathered for about a mile either side of Gore Cross before following a tractor towards the village.

One wonders what Matthew Dean would have made of the crowds passing the place where he was robbed 121 years

Imber as it is today

Richard Hooper leads a procession into the ruins of Imber.

before, or what Bob Watkin would have made of so many following the route his caravan of reddle-covered donkeys took year after year.

The protestors did their best, and national figures added their weight to the campaign. A message from John Betjeman read: 'Success to your campaign. Wiltshire and the rolling downs for ever. God save Imber.' But even the most ardent campaigners now accept that the village of Imber has joined the village of St John of Gore in history. The house where Alice Tinnams lived has been absorbed back into the Plain. The field where she played Kissing in the ring is now home to deadlier games but they, like Alice's game, will no doubt change, and pass in time. Curiously, but perhaps appropriately, it is the Army's presence that has granted Betjeman's wish for 'Wiltshire and the rolling downs for ever'. After all, high on the windswept Plain is a place for warriors.